Welcome to the *Write Source*!

This *Write Source* book was written just for you. We hope you have fun and learn, too.

Enjoy writing,
Your friends at the Write Source

Using the *Write Source* Book

Your *Write Source* book includes lessons and tips about writing. You will learn to write letters, reports, stories, poems, and more.

Besides writing, you will learn how to listen, speak, and take tests in class. Finally, a special section, called the "Proofreader's Guide," explains the rules of writing.

HOUGHTON MIFFLIN HARCOURT

WRITE SOURCE

Authors
Dave Kemper, Patrick Sebranek, and Verne Meyer

Illustrator
Chris Krenzke

GREAT
SOURCE®

 HOUGHTON MIFFLIN HARCOURT

Reviewers

Genevieve Bodnar NBCT
Youngstown City Schools
Youngstown, Ohio

Mary M. Fischer
Arlington Public Schools
Arlington, Massachusetts

Cynthia Fontenot
Green T. Lindon Elementary
Lafayette, Louisiana

Heather Hagstrum
Unified School District #475
Ft. Riley, Kansas

Lisa Kickbusch
Pattonville School District
St. Ann, Missouri

Michele A. Lewis
Pattonville School District
St. Ann, Missouri

Joyce Martin
Forest Ridge
    Elementary School
Howard County
Laurel, Maryland

Kim T. Mickle
Alief Independent
    School District
Houston, Texas

Lisa D. Miller
Greater Clark County Schools
Jeffersonville, Indiana

Karen A. Reid
Rosemead School District
Rosemead, California

Roslyn Rowley-Penk
Renton School District
Renton, Washington

Jeannine M. Shirley, M. Ed.
White Hall School District
White Hall, Arkansas

Tanya Smith
Frankford Elementary School
Frankford, Delaware

WRITE SOURCE Online
www.hmheducation.com/writesource

Printed in the U.S.A.

978-0-547-48496-9

1 2 3 4 5 6 7 8 9 10   0914   19 18 17 16 15 14 13 12 11 10

4500251395   A   B   C   D   E   F   G

Quick Guide

Contents

The Process of Writing

The Forms of Writing

Descriptive Writing

Narrative Writing

Expository Writing

Persuasive Writing

Responding to Literature

Creative Writing

Report Writing

The Tools of Learning

Basic Grammar and Writing

A Writer's Resource

Proofreader's Guide

Why Write?

The main reason to write is to communicate with others. Writing is an important way to share your feelings, thoughts, stories, and ideas.

Writing will help you . . .

- **Share with others.** You can tell your friends and family all about you in letters, cards, notes, and e-mail messages.

- **Remember more.** You can remember better when you write facts and ideas in your own words.

- **Learn more about you.** You will discover your own thoughts and feelings by writing.

- **Have fun.** You can imagine wonderful things in the stories, poems, and plays you write.

Remember: **The more you read, the better your writing will be.**

The Writing Process

Writing Focus

- Using the Writing Process
- Working with a Partner
- Writing Traits
- Rubric
- Publishing and Portfolios

Academic Vocabulary

Work with a partner. Read the meanings and share your answers.

1. A draft is a piece of writing that you have not finished yet.
   Why might you write a draft first?
2. A process is an order of steps.
   Tell the process of making a sandwich.
3. To create something means to make it.
   What can you create out of paper, scissors, and glue?

Writers do their work in many different ways. Tim slowly builds his stories, thinking carefully about each new idea. Gina finds it helpful to draw pictures as she writes. José likes to talk about his writing as he goes along. There are many ways to get ready to write.

In this part of the book, you will learn all about writing from using the writing process to publishing your writing.

Using the
Writing Process

Do you have stories to tell, reports to give, letters to send, invitations to write, and ideas to share? Well then, join us in learning about the writing process and see what you can create.

Talk it over.

1. What is your favorite piece of writing?
2. How did you write it?

Prewriting ▶ Planning Your Writing

When you prewrite, you **choose** your topic and **gather** details about it.

Writing ▶ Writing the First Draft

When you write a first draft, you **identify** your topic and **add** supporting details.

Revising ▶ Improving Your Writing

When you revise, you **change** parts to make your writing better. **Use** the traits of writing as a guide.

Editing ▶ Checking for Conventions

When you edit, you **check** for spelling, punctuation, and capitalization errors. Then you **correct** any that you find.

Publishing ▶ Sharing Your Final Copy

When you publish your writing, you **make** a neat, final copy and **share** it with others.

One Writer's Process

Monica's class had fun learning about holidays from around the world. Monica's teacher asked each student to write a paragraph about one of the holidays.

Follow along to see how Monica used the steps in the writing process to complete her paragraph.

Prewriting ▶ **Planning Your Writing**

When you prewrite, you choose your topic and gather details about it. You can use drawings during prewriting.

Choose   Monica decided to write about a special holiday in Japan, Children's Day.

Study   Monica remembered what she had learned about her topic in class. She also read about her topic.

Draw   Monica drew pictures of the details she wanted to write about.

Monica's Pictures

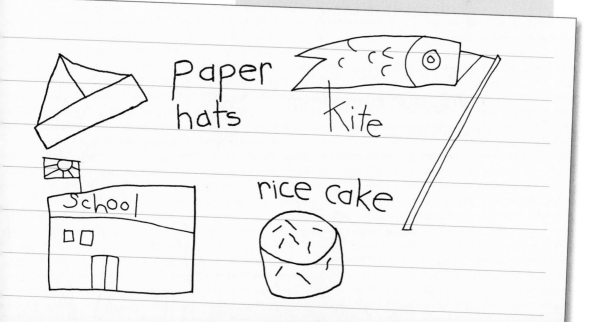

Writing ▶ Writing the First Draft

When you write your first draft, you put your ideas in sentence form.

These are the things Monica did to write her first draft.

Look Before she started writing, Monica looked at her drawings about Children's Day.

State In her first sentence, Monica told what she would write about.

Add Monica's next sentences added ideas and details about her topic.

> Most of the details in my paragraph come from my pictures.

Monica's First Draft

I lerned about Children's Day in school. It is a special day for the kids in Japan. They do fun stuff on this day. It comes on May 5. Children do not go to school on Children's Day they fly colorful fish kites from tall poles. They where paper hats and eat rice cakes. i think the fish kites would be fun to see. I wonder if rice cakes taste good.

Talk it over.

Which details from her pictures (page 7) did Monica include in her first draft?

Revising ▶ Improving Your Writing

When you revise, you try to improve your writing. You should change any parts that are unclear or hard to follow.

This is what Monica did to revise her paragraph.

Review   Monica read her first draft to herself.

Share   Next, Monica shared her first draft with a classmate.

Improve   Then she changed parts to improve her writing.

I moved one idea and replaced another one. I also added a new detail.

Monica's Revising

I lerned about Children's Day in

school. It is a special day for the kids

Children have fun

in Japan. ~~They do fun stuff~~ on this day.

(It comes on May 5.) Children do not

go to school on Children's Day they fly

colorful fish kites from tall poles. They

wrapped in leaves

where paper hats and eat rice cakes. i

think the fish kites would be fun to see. I

wonder if rice cakes taste good.

Talk it over.

What changes did Monica make?

Editing ▶ Checking for Conventions

When you edit, you check for correct spelling, punctuation, and capitalization.

This is what Monica did to edit her writing.

Read   Monica read her revised paragraph for conventions.

Correct   Monica corrected any capitalization, punctuation, and spelling mistakes she found.

Recheck   Monica checked her writing one last time for mistakes.

I used the editing marks listed inside the back cover of the book. I also added a title—Children's Day!

Monica's Editing

Children's Day

I ~~lerned~~ [learned] about Children's Day

in school. It comes on May 5. It is

a special day for the kids in Japan.

Children have fun on this day. Children

do not go to school on Children's Day.

they fly colorful fish kites from tall

poles. They ~~where~~ [wear] paper hats and eat

rice cakes wrapped in leaves. i think the

fish kites would be fun to see. I wonder

if rice cakes taste good.

Talk it over.

Which convention errors did Monica correct?

Publishing ▶ **Sharing Your Writing**

When you publish your writing, you make a final copy and share it with others.

This is what Monica did to publish her writing.

Complete Monica made a final copy of her paragraph. She skipped a line after her title and indented the first line of her paragraph. Monica included all of her changes and corrections.

Share Then Monica shared her paragraph by reading it out loud to her classmates.

I decided to draw a fish kite on my final copy.

Monica's Paragraph

Children's Day

(Skip)

(Indent) I learned about Children's Day in school. It comes on May 5. It is a special day for the kids in Japan. Children have fun on this day. Children do not go to school on Children's Day. They fly colorful fish kites from tall poles. They wear paper hats and eat rice cakes wrapped in leaves. I think the fish kites would be fun to see. I wonder if rice cakes taste good.

Talk it over.

1. What details in Monica's paragraph do you like the best? Name two.
2. What thoughts does Monica share in the last two sentences?

Working with a
Partner

In art class, Luis made a coil pot, and he decided to write a story about it. He shared his story with a partner. She asked some questions and that gave Luis some good ideas to make his story even better.

Helping One Another

Being a partner and having a partner is helpful as you go through the writing process.

Here are some ways partners can help one another during the writing process.

Talk Partners can talk about topics and details. Talking can help you **prewrite** and **write**.

Listen and Ask Partners can listen while a first draft is shared out loud. Partners ask questions to help **revise** the writing.

Check Partners can help check writing for conventions. Working together can help **edit** the writing.

Read Partners can read and enjoy a final copy. Reading is one way to **publish**.

Being on a Team

Working with a partner is like being on a team. After writing a first draft, one team member reads his or her writing out loud. The other member listens and responds to the writing.

Partner  Tips

When You Are the Writer

Tell why you chose your topic.
Read your writing to your partner.
Pay attention to your partner's comments.

When You Are the Listener

Look at your partner.
Listen carefully to the writing.
Respond to the writing.
1. **Tell** your partner what you like.
2. **Ask** any questions you may have.

Using a Response Sheet

You can also use a response sheet to review your partner's writing.

Laura's Response

Response Sheet

Writer: <u>Luis</u>   Listener: <u>Laura</u>

Title: <u>My Coil Pot</u>

1. One thing I like about your story:

   <u>I like the way you told about</u>

   <u>making the long snake of clay.</u>

2. One question I have about your story:

   <u>Who are you going to give the</u>

   <u>pot to?</u>

Understanding the
Writing Traits

You can use the **six traits of writing** listed below to help you do your best writing.

 Ideas — **Start with good ideas!**

 **Organization** — **Make your writing easy to follow.**

 **Voice** — **Sound like you are really interested in your topic.**

 **Word Choice** — **Choose your words carefully.**

 **Sentence Fluency** — **Use different lengths of sentences.**

 **Conventions** — **Follow the rules for writing.**

Ideas

Start with good ideas!

Alita likes writing about her family. She thinks of good topics and gathers interesting details.

Topic my baby sister

Details three months old

cries when she is hungry

wears pink and yellow

smiles at me

sleeps a lot

looks like my baby pictures

practice

1. In a writing notebook, write down an interesting topic and at least three important details about it.
2. Share your ideas with a partner.

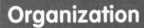

Organization

Make your writing easy to follow.

Cole makes sure that his writing has a beginning, a middle, and an ending.

Our Sailing Adventure

The **Beginning** names the topic.

Last summer, I had an adventure with my grandma. We went to the harbor in Baltimore to sail on a tall ship.

First, we pulled on ropes to help put up the sails. Then we sailed out to

The **Middle** adds details.

sea. Soon we couldn't even see land. Squawking seagulls flew around us. When the crew first fired a cannon, the noise and smoke scared me. Then I

The **Ending** shares my final thought.

started laughing.

Grandma and I had a great time. I can't wait for our next adventure.

Voice

Sound like you are really interested in your topic.

Julian is really interested in his topic because he is writing about his dog. He likes to share ideas about him.

My Buddy

I'm Julian, and my dog is my best buddy. Can you guess what his name is? That's right! It's Buddy.

Buddy eats strange things. He chews on rugs and bones. He likes liver. Once he even ate a raw fish. He smelled awful after that.

Buddy always spends time with me. Every morning, he walks me to the school bus. He's always waiting at the bus stop when I get home. At night, my best buddy sleeps on my bed.

practice

Write a story about an animal. Does your writing sound like you are really interested in your topic?

Word Choice

Choose your words carefully.

Riley uses specific words that make her writing clear and fun to read.

General Words (not clear)

A boy came **into the** room.

Specific Words (clear)

Marcus tiptoed **into the** kitchen.

Sentence Fluency

Use different lengths of sentences.

Jackson makes sure to use short and long sentences.

Rex barked. (short) He saw a rabbit and chased it across the yard. (long)

Conventions **Follow the rules for writing.**

Before Mia publishes her writing, she checks for capitalization, punctuation, and spelling. She uses a checklist to help her.

Did you check?

Capitalization

✓ 1. Did you start each sentence with a capital letter?

✓ 2. Did you capitalize the first letter of names?

Punctuation

✓ 3. Did you end each sentence with the correct punctuation mark?

Spelling

✓ 4. Did you spell all your words correctly?

Whenever you write, use the **six traits of good writing.**

Connecting the Process and the Traits

The writing process and the six traits of writing work together. The chart shows that some traits are important during certain steps in the process.

Prewrite

Ideas	Choose a topic and details.
Organization	Put your details in order.
Voice	Plan how to show interest in the topic.

Write

Ideas	Put your ideas on paper.
Organization	Make your ideas easy to follow.
Voice	Sound interested in your topic.

Revise

Ideas	Change any ideas that could be clearer.
Organization	Change or move parts that seem out of order.
Voice	Change parts that don't show interest.
Word Choice	Change words to be clear and specific.
Sentence Fluency	Change sentences to short and long.

Edit

Conventions	Check capitalization, punctuation, and spelling.

Writing Tips

- **Talk with a Partner**

  Talking with a partner will help you gather great ideas.

- **Use Graphic Organizers**

  Graphic organizers will help you organize your ideas.

- **Think About Your Reader**

  Think of your reader to help you find the right voice.

- **Check Your Sentences**

  Make sure your sentences are clear and easy to follow.

Don't worry about the conventions too early in the process. Leave that until you have revised your writing.

Using a
Rubric

Hana loves to look at the rabbits at the fair. Judges rate or score the rabbits according to their health and grooming. The very best rabbits get blue ribbons, and others get red or white ribbons.

Your writing can be scored, too, with a chart called a **rubric**. This chapter will show you how to rate your writing.

Getting Started

At the beginning of each main unit, you will see a "Goals for Writing" page. It shows you goals for four key traits of writing.

Sample Goals Page

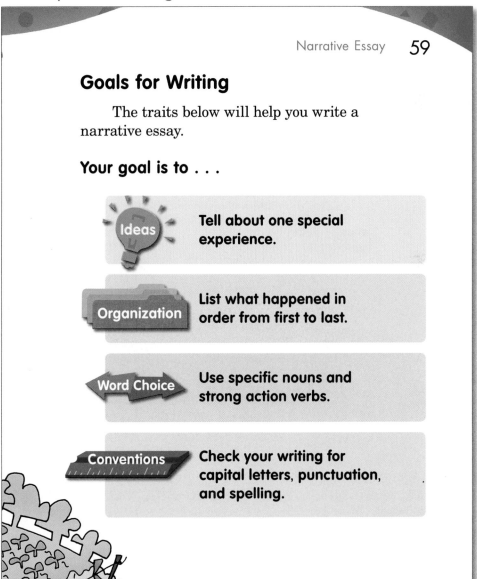

Goals for Writing

The traits below will help you write a narrative essay.

Your goal is to . . .

Ideas   Tell about one special experience.

Organization   List what happened in order from first to last.

Word Choice   Use specific nouns and strong action verbs.

Conventions   Check your writing for capital letters, punctuation, and spelling.

Learning About a Rubric

The information under each number in the rubric below can help you improve your writing. Each trait of writing can be scored.

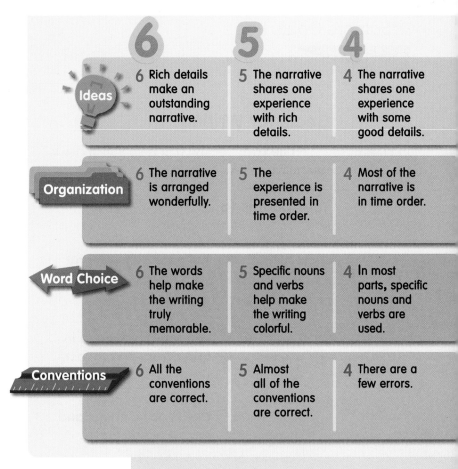

	6	**5**	**4**
Ideas	6 Rich details make an outstanding narrative.	5 The narrative shares one experience with rich details.	4 The narrative shares one experience with some good details.
Organization	6 The narrative is arranged wonderfully.	5 The experience is presented in time order.	4 Most of the narrative is in time order.
Word Choice	6 The words help make the writing truly memorable.	5 Specific nouns and verbs help make the writing colorful.	4 In most parts, specific nouns and verbs are used.
Conventions	6 All the conventions are correct.	5 Almost all of the conventions are correct.	4 There are a few errors.

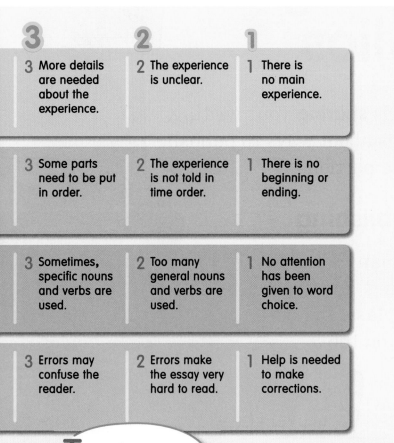

3

2

1

3 More details are needed about the experience.

2 The experience is unclear.

1 There is no main experience.

3 Some parts need to be put in order.

2 The experience is not told in time order.

1 There is no beginning or ending.

3 Sometimes, specific nouns and verbs are used.

2 Too many general nouns and verbs are used.

1 No attention has been given to word choice.

3 Errors may confuse the reader.

2 Errors make the essay very hard to read.

1 Help is needed to make corrections.

Talk it over.

1. Which traits are shown on this rubric?
2. Look at the ideas trait. How could you improve the ideas in your writing?

Publishing and Portfolios

Publishing is **sharing** your writing. This chapter tells about ways to publish, including using a portfolio.

Ideas for Publishing

There are many ways to share your writing. Kara reads the story to her class. Denzel puts his writing on the bulletin board.

More Publishing Ideas

Act it out!   Act out your story for your class, your
family, or friends.

Bind it!   Make a book. Put your writing and
pictures together in a book.

Send it!   Write an e-mail. Send it to a friend,
a family member, or a classmate.

Submit it!   Send your story to magazines that
publish student writing.

Display it!   With your teacher's permission, display
your writing in the classroom.

Read it!   Read your writing to classmates,
friends, and family. Sometimes the
simplest way to publish can be the best.

Talk it over.

What other ways can you think of to share
your writing?

Sharing a Handwritten Copy

When you write your final copy, remember these things.

- Use your best penmanship.
- Write on one side of your paper.
- Add a picture.

Handwritten Copy

Saturday

Saturday is the best day of the week. My family and I have breakfast together. Sometimes we have pancakes. Other times we have breakfast burritos. Then we might go shopping. Some Saturdays we go to the park to kick a ball around. It doesn't matter where we go. I love Saturdays!

Sharing a Computer Copy

When you use a computer, be sure that your writing looks neat and readable.

- Leave a one-inch margin on all sides.
- Use a font that is easy to read.
- Add a photo or a picture.

Computer Copy

↕ 1"

Saturday

Saturday is the best day of the week. My family and I have breakfast together. Sometimes we have pancakes. Other times we have breakfast burritos. Then we might go shopping. Some Saturdays we go to the park to kick a ball around. It doesn't matter where we go. I love Saturdays!

Understanding Portfolios

A **portfolio** is a special place to keep your writing. You can use a special folder for your portfolio, or you can use an electronic file on the computer. Your teacher will check your portfolio from time to time to see how you are doing.

Using a Portfolio

A portfolio can be used in many ways. Here are four important uses.

Collect You can collect ideas for new stories and poems.

Keep You can keep pictures and drawings you like.

Store You can store unfinished writing to work on later.

Save You can save final copies to read later.

Two Kinds of Portfolios

There are two main kinds of portfolios that you can create.

Showcase Portfolio

In a *showcase portfolio,* you show your best writing. Your teacher will help you decide which writing to include.

Growth Portfolio

In a *growth portfolio,* you save writing from different times of the year. You will be surprised how your writing improves.

Talk it over.

Which kind of portfolio would you like to make? Explain your answer.

Descriptive Writing

Writing Focus

- Descriptive Paragraph
- Across the Curriculum

Academic Vocabulary

Work with a partner. Read the meanings and share your answers.

1. A **descriptive** sentence describes what something looks like, sounds like, feels like, smells like, or tastes like.
   Tell your partner a descriptive sentence about your favorite animal.

2. A **curriculum** is a list of the subjects you study in school, such as math and science.
   What are your favorite subjects in your curriculum?

3. If you **review** something, you study it again carefully to see if changes are needed.
   What do you look for when you review your writing?

In descriptive writing, you use words to create a picture, or image, for a topic. You can tell what your topic looks like, sounds like, feels like, smells like, or tastes like—just by sharing the best words and details.

Literature Connections: You can find descriptive language in *South Korea* by Susan E. Haberle.

Writing a
Descriptive
Paragraph

Isabel described her friend Marty in a descriptive paragraph. In a way, she painted a picture with words. You can make a word picture of someone you know, too! This chapter will show you how.

Isabel's Descriptive Paragraph

My Teammate Marty

Topic Sentence

My friend Marty is on my soccer team. He wears a blue baseball hat. His hair is dark brown, and his eyes light up when he smiles. He wears a uniform that includes a T-shirt and blue pants. Marty's white shoes wear out quickly because he runs fast and plays hard. Marty loves playing soccer, and he is a great teammate.

Body Sentences

Closing Sentence

- The **topic sentence** tells who the paragraph is about.
- The **body sentences** describe what the person looks like and what she or he does.
- The **closing sentence** tells how the writer feels about the person.

Prewriting ▶ Planning Your Writing

To get started you need to select an interesting topic and gather details about it.

First, Isabel listed interesting people she knows. Then she circled the person she wanted to write about.

After Isabel chose Marty as her topic, she created a chart of details about him.

Quick List

Grandma Vi

Anita

Marty

Details Chart

Topic: Marty		
Looks like	Sounds like	Likes to do
big smile	soft voice	loves soccer
red striped shirt	giggles	runs fast
blue cap		likes popcorn

Prewrite ▶ Choose a topic/Gather details.

1. List three people you know well.
2. Circle one person to write about.
3. Make a details chart like the one above.
4. Draw a picture of your person, if it will help you.

Writing ▶ Writing Your First Draft

You can use your details chart and picture to help you write your paragraph. Remember each part of your paragraph has a special job.

> Isabel wrote a topic sentence, body sentences, and a closing sentence in her paragraph. She used many ideas from her details chart.

Write ▶ **Write your first draft.**

1. Write your **topic sentence**.

> Write your own sentence or use the form that follows.

My friend _____(name)_____ is _____(special detail)_____.

2. Write your **body sentences**. Use words and details from your chart and picture to describe the person.
3. Write your **closing sentence**. Tell how you feel about the person.

Revising ▶ Improving Your Writing

Now it is time to review your writing to see if any parts need to be improved. When you revise, check for the traits your teacher feels are really important.

For her revising, Isabel focused special attention on her word choices and sentence fluency.

Isabel changed some words and used sentences of different lengths.

Revise ▶ Improve your writing.

1. Change general words to specific words.

My friend Marty is on my~team.
soccer

Marty wears a hat.
blue baseball hat

2. Use sentences of different lengths.

Marty's white shoes wear out quickly. He runs fast and plays hard.
because

Editing ▶ Checking for Conventions

After you revise your paragraph, check it for capitalization, punctuation, and spelling.

Isabel and a classmate checked her writing for conventions, using the checklist below as a guide.

Isabel's Editing

My friend Marty is on my soccer ~~teem~~ (*team*).

He wears a blue baseball hat⊙ ~~h~~ **H**is hair is dark

brown, and his eyes light up when he smiles.

Did you check?

✓ 1. Did you begin each sentence with a capital letter?

✓ 2. Did you end each sentence with correct punctuation?

✓ 3. Did you spell your words correctly?

Edit ▶ Check for errors.

Writing
Across the Curriculum
Science or Math: A Shape Riddle

In science or math class, you may be asked to write about subjects you are studying. Ronnie wrote a shape riddle for his science class.

What Am I?

The **topic sentence** names the helper.

I am a sphere in room 213.

I feel round and smooth like a ball.

I am bigger than a basketball. Some

The **body sentences** give clues.

parts of me are blue. Other parts

are brown or green. I have words

and lines all over me. I can show you

The **closing sentence** asks the riddle question.

where anyone on Earth lives. What

am I?

Answer: a globe

Writing Tips

Before You Write

Details Chart

Pick an object that has a special shape.

Complete a details chart about the object.

Topic:		
Looks like	Sounds like	Know about

During Your Writing

Name your object's shape in the topic sentence.

Give clues from your list in the body sentences.

In the closing, write your riddle question.

After You Have Written

Read your riddle to a partner to see if it makes sense.

Add or change details to make your riddle clear.

Correct mistakes and make a final copy.

Practical Writing: An E-Mail Message

Paul wrote an e-mail message to his friend Jo. He talked about a park near his home in Florida.

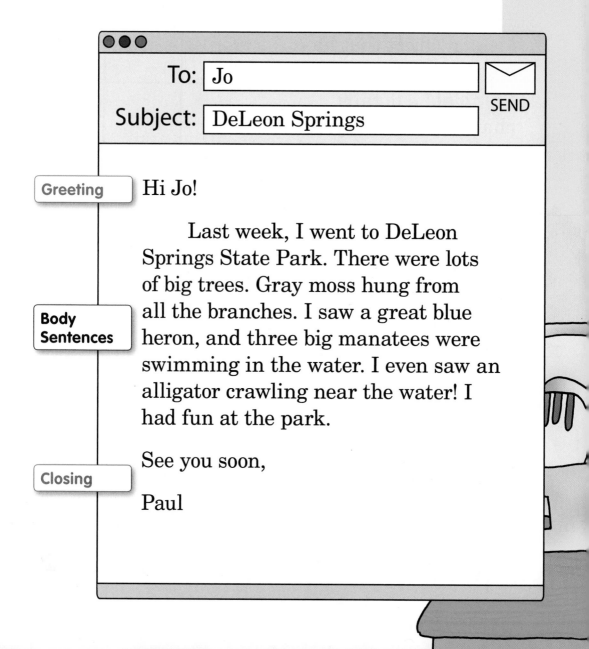

To: Jo

Subject: DeLeon Springs

SEND

Greeting

Hi Jo!

Body Sentences

Last week, I went to DeLeon Springs State Park. There were lots of big trees. Gray moss hung from all the branches. I saw a great blue heron, and three big manatees were swimming in the water. I even saw an alligator crawling near the water! I had fun at the park.

Closing

See you soon,

Paul

Writing Tips

Before You Write

Choose a person to receive your e-mail.

Pick a place to describe.

Make a sensory list to gather details.

Sensory List

See	
Hear	
Smell	
Taste	
Feel	

During Your Writing

Begin with a fun greeting.

Share ideas from your list in the body sentences.

Make your closing a friendly good-bye.

After You Have Written

Read over your e-mail. Be sure you have clearly described your place.

Correct mistakes in capitalization, punctuation, and spelling.

Send your e-mail.

Narrative Writing

Writing Focus

- Narrative Paragraph
- Narrative Essay
- Across the Curriculum
- Assessment

Academic Vocabulary

Work with a partner. Read the meanings and share your answers.

1. A time line shows events in time order.
   On a time line of your life, what event would you list first?
2. A narrative is a story.
   Tell a narrative of your day so far.
3. An experience is something that you do.
   What kind of experience have you had shopping in a store?

You like to tell stories about interesting or important things that happen to you, right? When you write those stories down, they're called narratives. In a narrative, you can tell what happened two years ago or what happened just last night. This section will help you write great narratives.

Literature Connections: You can find narrative writing in *My Name is Gabriela* by Monica Brown.

Writing a
Narrative
Paragraph

The students in Colin's class talked about special experiences. They discovered many stories that they could tell about themselves, their families, and their friends. Colin remembered visiting the zoo with his brother and decided to write a narrative paragraph about it.

In this chapter, you will write a paragraph about a special experience you've had.

Colin's Narrative Paragraph

My Zoo Surprise

Topic Sentence

    My big brother and I had fun at the zoo. The peacocks squawked and fanned out their tails. Prairie dogs chased each other and dived into their holes. Then we

Body Sentences

squeezed between people to get to a huge window where we could see underwater. Suddenly a polar bear crashed into the water. It pushed its nose right up to the window. My big

Closing Sentence

brother and I were nose to nose with a polar bear!

- The **topic sentence** tells the main idea of the paragraph.
- The **body sentences** tell what happened.
- The **closing sentence** gives the reader something to think about.

Prewriting ▶ Choosing Your Topic

When planning a paragraph, start by choosing an interesting topic.

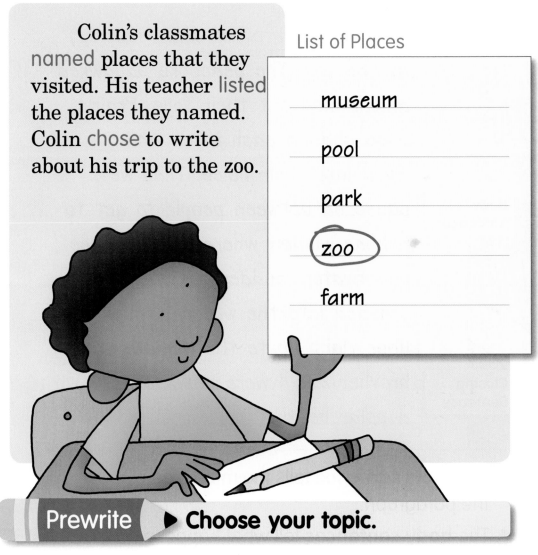

Colin's classmates named places that they visited. His teacher listed the places they named. Colin chose to write about his trip to the zoo.

List of Places

museum

pool

park

zoo

farm

Prewrite ▶ **Choose your topic.**

1. List some places you've visited.
2. Choose a place and a time to write about.

Gathering Details

The next important step is to select details about your topic.

To gather details, Colin made a time line. He listed events in the order they happened. This is called *time order*.

Time Line

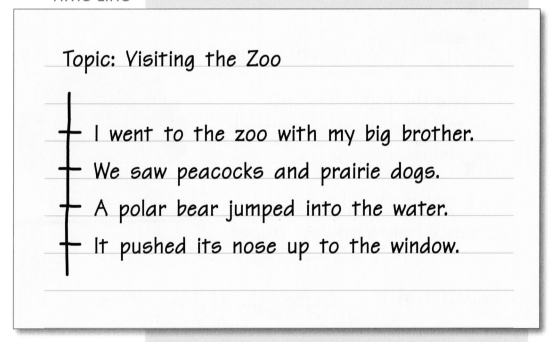

Topic: Visiting the Zoo

┼ I went to the zoo with my big brother.
┼ We saw peacocks and prairie dogs.
┼ A polar bear jumped into the water.
┼ It pushed its nose up to the window.

Prewrite ▶ **Gather details.**

1. Make a time line like the one above.
2. List the main events of your story in time order.

Writing ▶ Writing Your Paragraph

Now you are ready to write your narrative paragraph. Use your time line as a guide.

To begin, Colin wrote a topic sentence that tells what his paragraph is about. He then added sentences that tells his story. Collin closed with an interesting idea.

Write ▶ **Write your paragraph.**

1. Write the topic sentence to tell what your paragraph is about.

If you get stuck, fill in the sentence below on your paper.

I had fun with _____(person)_____ at the __(place)__ .

2. Add sentences to tell your story.
3. Close with a sentence that gives a final interesting or fun idea.

Revising and Editing

Once you finish your first draft, you are ready to revise and edit it. Your goal is to make your paragraph clear and fun to read.

> Colin reviewed his ideas to make sure they are in the right order and interesting. Then he checked his paragraph for conventions.

Revise ▶ Improve your writing.

1. Be sure the events in your story are in the right order.
2. Also decide if your story sounds interesting.

Edit ▶ Check for conventions.

1. Be sure that you use capital letters and punctuation correctly.
2. Also check for spelling errors.

Writing a
Narrative Essay

Fred helped his grandpa in a community garden. He wrote about his adventure in a narrative essay. A narrative essay uses more than one paragraph to tell about a true experience.

In this chapter, you will write a narrative essay about an adventure at a special place.

Goals for Writing

The traits below will help you write a narrative essay.

Your goal is to . . .

Ideas — Tell about one special experience.

Organization — List what happened in order from first to last.

Word Choice — Use specific nouns and strong action verbs.

Conventions — Check your writing for capital letters, punctuation, and spelling.

Fred's Narrative Essay

My Day at the Community Garden

Beginning   My grandpa took me to the community garden. It contains rows and rows of healthy plants.

Middle   Grandpa showed me leaf lettuce, snap peas, and sweet corn. Then he showed me how to pull weeds without pulling the vegetables. It's not easy. He told me that garden work is important. He said, "People who have food need to share it." Finally, we took the food from the garden to a food bank. I felt proud working with Grandpa.

Ending   Now I know about growing vegetables and pulling weeds. The best part was spending time with Grandpa. I learned that working together and helping others is fun.

Parts of an Essay

An essay contains three main parts—the beginning, the middle, and the ending. Look at the three parts of Fred's essay.

In the beginning paragraph, Fred tells which special experience he will write about.

In the middle paragraph, Fred writes about the experience.

In the ending paragraph, Fred explains what he learned and how he feels.

After You Read

1. **Ideas** What experience did Fred share?
2. **Organization** What order did Fred use to tell about his day with his grandfather?
3. **Word Choice** What sentence contains specific nouns?

Prewriting ▶ Choosing a Topic

Choosing a topic is the important first step when planning a narrative. Always select a writing topic that really interests you.

Here's how Kelsey selected her topic.

List Kelsey listed places she had been.

Circle She then circled the topic she wanted to write about.

List of Places

hospital

(Standing Rock)

Navy Pier

zoo

Prewrite ▶ **Choose a topic.**

1. List places you have visited.
2. Circle the place you want to write about.

Gathering Details

Before writing, it is important to collect details about your topic.

This is how Kelsey collected her details.

Make   Kelsey made a cluster.

Name   She named her topic in the middle of her cluster. Then she added details.

Details Cluster

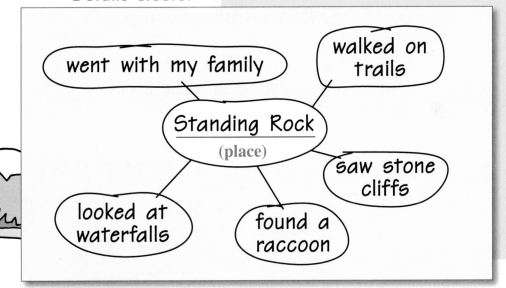

went with my family

walked on trails

Standing Rock
(place)

saw stone cliffs

looked at waterfalls

found a raccoon

Prewrite ▶ **Gather details.**

1. Make a cluster.
2. Name your topic and add details about it.

Writing ▶ Beginning Your Story

The beginning part of a narrative should get the reader's interest and introduce your topic.

This is what Kelsey did to write the beginning of her story.

▶ Beginning
Middle
Ending

Review Kelsey reviewed the ideas in her cluster.

Write Then Kelsey wrote a beginning sentence that introduces her topic.

My family and I went to Standing Rock state park.

Add Next, Kelsey wrote more sentences to help introduce her topic.

Kelsey's beginning paragraph introduces her topic and leads up to the main action in her story.

Kelsey's Beginning Paragraph

> My family and I went to Standing Rock state park. Waterfalls fell over some of the high rocks. We were walking along the trail through stone clifs. I saw fuzzy green stuff on the edge of the path Then I yelled, "I hear something really strange!"

Write ▶ **Begin your story.**

1. Write an interesting sentence to introduce your topic.
2. Add more sentences to help introduce the topic.

Writing ▶ Continuing Your Story

In the middle part of your narrative, you should tell about the main action. Make this part exciting!

This is what Kelsey did to continue her story.

Review Kelsey again looked at her cluster for ideas to include in the middle part of her story.

Write Next, she wrote about the main action.

Include Kelsey included details, dialogue (talking), and personal feelings.

> I used quotation marks to show that someone is talking.

In the middle paragraph, Kelsey included details, dialogue, and her personal feelings.

Kelsey's Middle Paragraph

Inside a garbage can, I found a raccoon. We see wild animals in our backyard. "There's a baby raccoon here!" I shouted. I was mad because no one beleved me. Who cared about seeing another waterfall? I wanted to help the little raccoon. Dad and Mom just wanted to keep walking.

Write ▶ Continue your story.

1. Review your cluster for ideas.
2. Write about the main action of your story.
3. Include details, dialogue, and personal feelings.

Writing ▶ Ending Your Story

In the ending part, you should finish your story and tell one last important thing.

This is what Kelsey did to write her ending.

| Beginning |
| Middle |
| ▶ Ending |

Write Kelsey finished her story by telling how the main action ended.

Add Kelsey added her last sentence. She tried three ways to write it.

1. **Say something about yourself.**

   I learned I could be a hero!

2. **Say something about other people.**

   Park workers have an important job.

3. **State the final idea about the topic.**

   Wild animals like to be free.

Kelsey's ending paragraph completes her story and shares a final idea.

Kelsey's Ending Paragraph

> We finally got back from hiking. Dad looked in the garbage can and saw my raccoon! Then he found a park worker. She tipped the can over and the raccoon hurried into the woods. I learned that I could be a hero!

In my last sentence, I decided to share what I learned about myself.

Write ▶ **End your story.**

1. Write the final part to finish your story.
2. Add one more sentence to complete the narrative.

Revising ▶ Improving Your Ideas

When you revise, you try to make your story better. First, make sure you have used the best ideas.

These are the things that Kelsey did to improve the ideas in her story.

Ideas

Read Kelsey read her first draft to herself and to a partner.

Reading your story out loud helps you find ideas that should be changed.

Listen She listened to what her partner said about her ideas.

Make Then Kelsey made any needed changes.

In the beginning paragraph, I added two details to make my writing clearer.

Kelsey's Revising

Last summer,
∧My family and I went to Standing
Rock state park. Waterfalls fell over
some of the high rocks. We were
walking along the ∧trail through stone
narrow
clifs. I saw fuzzy green stuff on the
edge of the path Then I yelled, "I hear
something really strange!"

Revise ▶ Improve your ideas.

1. Read your first draft to yourself and to a partner.
2. Listen to what your partner says about your ideas.
3. Make any needed changes.

Revising ▶ Improving Your Organization

When you revise for organization, you make sure that your ideas are in the best order.

These are the things that Kelsey did to check her writing for organization.

Organization

Review   Kelsey reviewed her first draft for organization.
1. She made sure she included a beginning, a middle, and an ending.
2. She also made sure that her sentences were in the best order.

Make   Kelsey then made any needed changes.

In the first paragraph, I decided to move one sentence to make my writing clearer.

Kelsey's Revising

Last summer,
        ∧My family and I went to Standing

Rock state park. Waterfalls fell over

some of the high rocks. We were
                narrow
walking along the ∧trail through stone

clifs. I saw fuzzy green stuff on the

edge of the path Then I yelled, "I hear

something really strange!"

Make sure your story is easy to follow from start to finish.

Revise ▶ **Improve your organization.**

1. Review your first draft for organization.
2. Make any needed changes.

Revising ▶ Improving Your Word Choice

When you revise for word choice, you make sure that your words are specific and colorful.

Word Choice

These are the things that Kelsey did to revise her writing for word choice.

Review Kelsey again reviewed her first draft. She paid careful attention to the words.

Mark She marked the words she wanted to change with the take out (⟍) editing symbol.

Decide Kelsey then decided on better words to use in those places.

In the first paragraph, I changed two nouns and one verb to make them stronger.

Thesaurus

Kelsey used a thesaurus to find better words.

Kelsey's Revising

Last summer, **parents**
$\wedge$My ~~family~~ and I went to Standing

Rock state park. Waterfalls fell over

some of the high rocks. We were
hiking   **narrow**
~~walking~~ along the $\wedge$trail through stone
                              moss
clifs. I saw fuzzy green ~~stuff~~ on the

edge of the path Then I yelled, "I hear

something really strange!"

Revise ▶ **Improve your word choice.**

1. Review your first draft for word choice.
2. Mark the words you want to change using the take out (___✗) editing symbol.
3. Decide on new words to use in those places.

Editing ▸ Checking for Conventions

After revising your first draft, it's time to check it for capitalization, punctuation, and spelling.

These are the things that Kelsey did to edit her writing for conventions.

Conventions

Check Kelsey checked her story for conventions. She used the checklist below as a guide.

Ask She also asked a classmate to check her story for conventions.

Mark Then Kelsey marked her errors and corrected them.

Did you check?

✔ 1. Did you capitalize names and the first word of each sentence?

✔ 2. Did you use punctuation at the end of each sentence?

✔ 3. Did you add quotation marks around a speaker's words?

✔ 4. Did you spell your words correctly?

Kelsey's Editing

Last summer, my parents and

I went to Standing Rock state park.
                              S   P

We were hiking along the narrow trail

through stone clifs. Waterfalls fell
         cliffs

over some of the high rocks. I saw

fuzzy green moss on the edge of the

path. Then I yelled, "I hear something

really strange!"

> I added capital letters to the name of a place, corrected a spelling error, and added a period.

Edit ▶ **Check for conventions.**

1. Check your story for conventions using the checklist.
2. Ask a partner to check for conventions, too.
3. Mark any errors and correct them.

Publishing ▶ Sharing Your Essay

Standing Rock State Park

Last summer, my parents and I went to Standing Rock State Park. We walked on trails through stone cliffs. Waterfalls fell over high rocks. I saw fuzzy green moss on the edge of the path. Then I yelled, "I hear something really strange!"

Inside a garbage can, I found a raccoon. "There's a baby raccoon here!" I yelled. Dad and Mom just wanted to keep walking. I was mad because no one believed me. Who cared about seeing another waterfall? I wanted to help the little raccoon!

We finally got back from hiking. Dad looked in the garbage can and saw my raccoon! Then Dad found a park ranger. She tipped the can over, and the raccoon hurried into the woods. I learned that I could be a hero!

Publish ▶ Share your essay.

Reflecting on Your Writing

After you finish your essay, take some time to think about it. Then fill in a sheet like this about your story.

Thinking About Your Writing

Name: _Kelsey_

Title: _Standing Rock State Park_

1. The best thing about my essay is

   remembering the baby raccoon in

   the garbage can.

2. The main thing I learned while writing my essay is _how to use quotation_

   marks around dialogue.

Using a Rubric

The rubric on these pages can help you rate your writing.

Great!

6   5   4

Ideas

6 Rich details make an outstanding narrative.

5 The narrative shares one experience with rich details.

4 The narrative shares one experience with some good details.

Organization

6 The narrative is arranged wonderfully.

5 The experience is presented in time order.

4 Most of the narrative is in time order.

Word Choice

6 The words help make the writing truly memorable.

5 Specific nouns and verbs help make the writing colorful.

4 In most parts, specific nouns and verbs are used.

Conventions

6 All the conventions are correct.

5 Almost all of the conventions are correct.

4 There are a few errors.

Literature Connections: You can find narrative writing in *Gloria Who Might Be My Best Friend* by Ann Cameron.

Keep Trying!

3   **2**   **1**

3 More details are needed about the experience.	2 The experience is unclear.	1 There is no main experience.
3 Some parts need to be put in order.	2 The experience is not told in time order.	1 There is no beginning or ending.
3 Sometimes, specific nouns and verbs are used.	2 Too many general nouns and verbs are used.	1 No attention has been given to word choice.
3 Errors may confuse the reader.	2 Errors make the essay very hard to read.	1 Help is needed to make corrections.

Writing
Across the Curriculum

Social Studies: A Community Helper

For social studies, Josie wrote a story about a community helper. She chose to write about a crossing guard.

Ms. Stein to the Rescue

Topic Sentence

Ms. Stein is our school crossing guard. One day, I was waiting for Ms. Stein to let me cross. Just then, a puppy ran into the street. I yelled to Ms.

Body Sentences

Stein. Then she saw the puppy, too. She told me to stay where I was. Ms. Stein stepped into the street and held up her stop sign. All the cars stopped, and Ms. Stein picked up the puppy.

Closing Sentence

I felt proud because she said, "Good job, you helped me save the puppy's life."

Writing Tips

Before You Write

List some community helpers.

Think about an experience you shared with one of them.

Use a time line to gather details about the experience.

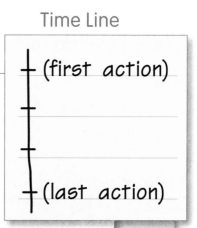

Time Line

(first action)

(last action)

During Your Writing

Name the helper in the topic sentence.

Tell about the experience in the body sentences.

Share how you felt in the closing sentence.

After You Have Written

Review your paragraph.

Add or change any parts to make them clearer.

Check for conventions.

Music: A Personal Story

For music class, Richard wrote a story about playing in a family band. The band played zydeco music.

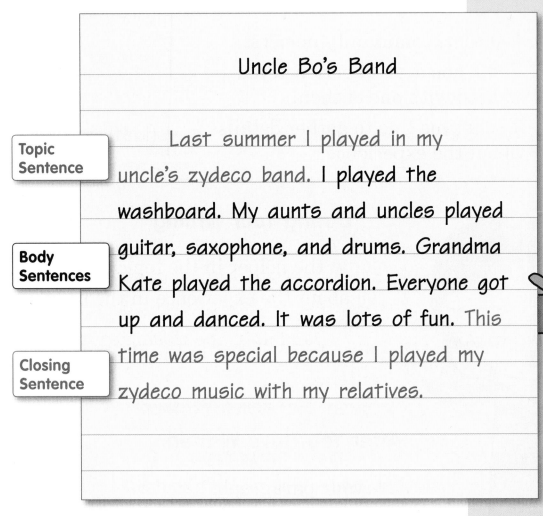

Uncle Bo's Band

Topic Sentence

Last summer I played in my uncle's zydeco band. I played the washboard. My aunts and uncles played guitar, saxophone, and drums. Grandma Kate played the accordion. Everyone got up and danced. It was lots of fun. This time was special because I played my zydeco music with my relatives.

Body Sentences

Closing Sentence

Writing Tips

Before You Write

List experiences you have had with music.

Choose one of the times to write about.

Use a cluster to gather details about the experience.

Cluster

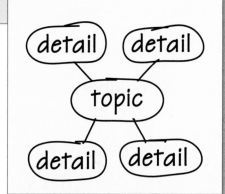

During Your Writing

Name the experience in the topic sentence.

Tell what happened in the body sentences.

Share how you felt in the closing sentence.

After You Have Written

Review your paragraph.

Make sure you wrote about one special time.

Check for conventions.

Writing for Assessment

On most writing tests, you will read a **prompt** and write a paragraph about it.

Writing Prompt

> Remember something you did for the first time. Write a paragraph about the time.

Think After Zane read the prompt, he thought about things that he'd done for the first time.

List He listed a few of those experiences.

Choose Zane chose the experience he wanted to write about and circled it.

List of Experiences

trampoline
high board
soccer goal

Zane's Narrative Paragraph

The **topic sentence** names the topic.

The **body sentences** tell what happened.

The **closing sentence** shares a feeling.

My High Jump

Last summer, Aunt Shandi took me to a pool. Kids in the water were splashing, swimming, and yelling. Then I saw the high diving board. I'd never used it before, but Aunt Shandi said I could jump. I climbed up the big ladder. The water looked a long way down. I took a deep breath and jumped. Down I went. The water made a great big splash around me. My jump was great!

practice

1. List first-time experiences.
2. Write a paragraph about one of your first-time experiences.

Expository Writing

www.hmheducation.com/writesource

Writing Focus

- Expository Paragraph
- Expository Essay
- Across the Curriculum
- Assessment

Academic Vocabulary

Work with a partner. Read the meanings and share your answers.

1. **Directions** tell how to do something.
   Give directions for making a snack.

2. When you **restate** something, you say it again, or you say it in a different way.
   Restate the directions you gave for making a snack.

3. If you **select** something, you choose it from a number of things.
   What food would you select if you went out to eat?

Expository writing is writing that explains or gives information. Reports, recipes, and invitations are examples of expository writing. In this section, you will write directions, a how-to essay, a classroom report, and an invitation. To do your best work, be sure to know a lot about each of your topics.

 Literature Connections: You can find an example of expository writing in *How to Make a Kite* by Joanna Korba.

Writing an
Expository
Paragraph

Directions come in all shapes and sizes. You find directions in cookbooks. You also find them to help you make models or play new games.

To help a new student, Max and his classmates wrote directions to different places in their school. You can write directions, too. This chapter will show you how.

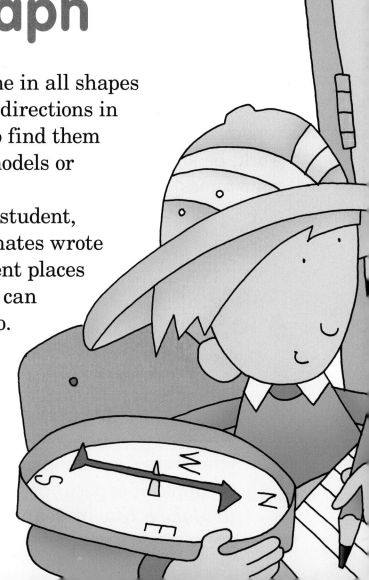

Max's Expository Paragraph

How to Find the Lunchroom

Topic Sentence

It is easy to get from our classroom to the lunchroom. First, you leave our classroom and turn left. Walk past the office. Then

Body Sentences

go to the trophy case, turn right, and stop. Look straight ahead of you to the end of the hall. What

Closing Sentence

do you see? You've found the lunchroom!

- The **topic sentence** introduces the topic.
- The **body sentences** give step-by-step directions.
- The **closing sentence** restates the main idea.

Prewriting ▶ Choosing a Topic

When planning an expository paragraph, begin by selecting a topic that you really want to write about.

Max listed the places that a new student would need to find. He chose to write directions for getting from his classroom to the lunchroom.

What are some important places in your school?

List of Places

gym

office

lunchroom

art room

library

playground

Prewrite ▶ Choose your topic.

1. List several places in your school.
2. Choose one place for writing directions.

Gathering Details

After you select a topic, gather details about it for your directions.

Max drew a map to help him remember details for his directions. His map shows how to get from his classroom to the lunchroom. He added labels to make his map clear.

Map

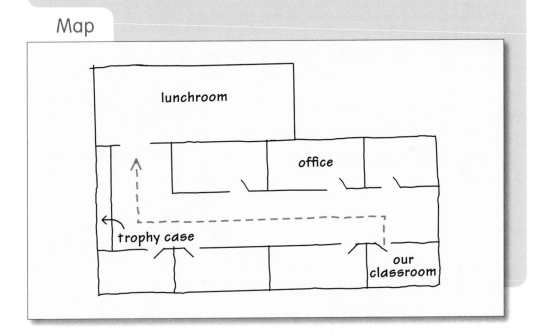

Prewrite ▶ **Gather your details.**

1. Draw a map that shows the route from your classroom to your topic.
2. Label at least one place you pass on the way.

Writing ▸ **Writing the First Draft**

Now you are ready to write your expository paragraph. Be sure to use your map as a guide.

> First, Max wrote a topic sentence that names the topic. He then explained his directions. He ended with a sentence that finishes the directions.

Write ▸ **Write your first draft.**

1. Write your topic sentence to introduce your topic.
2. Explain your directions.
3. End with a sentence that restates the main idea.

To start or end your paragraph, you may want to complete these sentences on your own paper.

To Start ▸ This is how to get to the ____(place)____ from the ____(place)____ .

To End ▸ You found the ____(place)____ !

Revising and Editing

Once you finish your first draft, you are ready to revise and edit it. Your goal is to make your directions easy to follow.

Max first made sure that he included all the directions in the right order. Then Max checked his paragraph for conventions.

Revise ▶ Improve your writing.

1. Be sure that you have included all of the directions.
2. Also make sure that your directions are in the right order.

Edit ▶ Check your conventions.

1. Be sure that you use capital letters and punctuation correctly.
2. Check for spelling errors.

Remember to indent the first line in your paragraph.

Publish ▶ Share your writing.

Writing an
Expository Essay

Emily likes to string beads. Maria knows how to grow flowers, and Ty flies kites. Everyone has a special activity that is enjoyable. What do you enjoy doing?

In this chapter, you will write an expository essay in which you explain how to do something.

Goals for Writing

The traits below will help you write a expository essay.

Your goal is to . . .

Ideas   Choose a how-to topic and explain it.

Organization   Put the steps in the right order.

Voice   Be sure that you sound interested and confident.

Conventions   Check your capitalization, punctuation, and spelling.

Ty's Expository Essay

How to Fly a Kite

Beginning   Flying a kite is fun and easy. You will need a kite, a kite tail, string, and a windy day. You should also find a big, open place to fly your kite.

Middle   First, stand with your back to the wind. Next, have a friend hold up the kite. When the wind blows, your friend should let go of the kite. Then run fast and let out some string. If the kites rises, let out even more string. If your kite crashes, just try again.

Ending   Flying a kite is the best! You never know how high or how far your kite will go.

Parts of an Essay

An essay contains three main parts—the beginning, the middle, and the ending. Look at the three parts of Ty's essay.

Beginning

Middle

Ending

The first paragraph names the topic and tells the reader what supplies are needed.

The middle paragraph explains how to do the activity.

The last paragraph tells why the activity is fun.

After You Read

1. **Ideas** What details teach you how to fly a kite? Name two.
2. **Organization** What words did Ty use to put the steps in order?
3. **Voice** Does Ty really like his topic? Name one sentence to show Ty's interest.

Prewriting ▶ Choosing a Topic

To get started, first choose a topic that you like and can explain.

Here's how Maria selected a topic for her expository essay.

List Maria made a list of activities she likes to do.

Circle She then circled the activity she wanted to write about.

What is your best activity?

List of Activities

wash my dog

grow a flower

play soccer

draw

ride bikes

Prewrite ▶ **Choose your topic.**

1. List activities you like to do.
2. Circle the activity you want to explain in an essay.

Gathering Details

To explain your activity, you will need to think of the steps needed to complete it. Be sure that you put the steps in the correct order.

Here's what Maria did to collect details for her expository essay.

Draw Maria drew pictures of the steps and numbered the steps.

Add Finally, Maria added words for each step.

Step-by-Step Pictures

Prewrite ▶ **Gather details.**

1. Draw pictures of the steps and number them.
2. Add words for each step.

Writing ▶ Beginning Your Essay

The beginning paragraph of your essay should introduce your topic in an interesting way. It should also name the supplies needed for the activity.

This is what Maria did to write the beginning of her essay.

▶ Beginning

Middle

Ending

Review Maria reviewed her pictures about the activity.

Introduce For her first sentences, she tried two ways to introduce her topic.

1. **Ask a question about the activity.**

   Would you like to grow a flower?

2. **Make a statement about the activity.**

   I can teach you how to grow a flower.

Add Maria's next sentences named the supplies needed for the activity.

Maria's beginning paragraph introduces her activity and names the supplies she used.

Maria's Beginning Paragraph

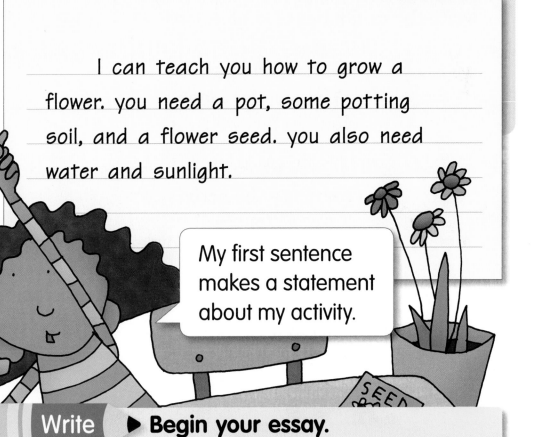

I can teach you how to grow a flower. you need a pot, some potting soil, and a flower seed. you also need water and sunlight.

My first sentence makes a statement about my activity.

Write ▶ **Begin your essay.**

1. Review your pictures.
2. Introduce your topic.
3. Add sentences that name the important supplies.

Writing ▶ Developing the Middle Part

In the middle part of your essay, you explain the steps to complete your activity. Be sure to use **time-order words** to make the steps easy to follow.

This is what Maria did to write the middle part of her essay.

Beginning
▶ **Middle**
Ending

Look Maria looked again at her pictures for ideas to include in her writing.

Explain Next, she explained the steps needed to complete the activity.

Include Maria included time-order words like *next, then, now,* and *soon.*

Use your pictures as a guide as you write.

In the middle paragraph, Maria explained how to do her activity. She used the time-order words.

Maria's Middle Paragraph

> Put some potting soil in a clay pot. Next, make a little hole in the dirt. Plant a seed. Cover it up with dirt. Now put the pot near a sunny window. Then give the seed a little water every day. Soon, a tiny, green plant will grow. Be sure it gets sunlight and water. A flower will bloum.

Write ▶ Develop the middle part.

1. Look at your pictures.
2. Explain the steps to complete the activity.
3. Include time-order words to connect the steps.

Writing ▶ Ending Your Essay

In the ending paragraph, you should state why you like the activity. Then you should give reasons to explain the statement.

This is what Maria did to write her ending paragraph.

Beginning

Middle

▶ Ending

Write Maria tried two ways to start this paragraph.

1. **Tell why you like the activity.**

   I like growing flowers because they are pretty.

2. **Tell why others might like this activity.**

   Growing flowers is a colorful hobby.

Choose Maria chose the best way.

Add Maria added two reasons that explain her choice.

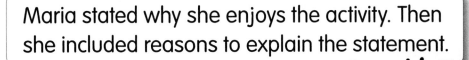

Maria stated why she enjoys the activity. Then she included reasons to explain the statement.

Maria's Ending Paragraph

I like growing flowers because they are pretty. It is fun to watch them grow. When they bloum, I pick them for my mom.

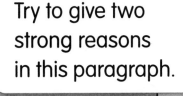

Try to give two strong reasons in this paragraph.

Write ▶ **End your essay.**

1. Write a sentence that tells why you like the activity or why the reader might like it.

2. Add two or three good reasons to explain the first sentence.

Revising ▶ Improving Your Ideas

When you revise, you try to make your essay better. First, be sure that you have used the best ideas.

These are the things that Maria did to improve the ideas in her essay.

Ideas

Read Maria read her first draft to herself and to a partner.

Listen She listened to what her partner said about her ideas.

Make Then Maria made the needed changes.

In the beginning paragraph, I added a detail. In the middle paragraph, I made an idea clearer.

Maria's Revising

I can teach you how to grow a
flower. you need a ~clay~ pot, some potting soil,
and a flower seed. you also need water
and sunlight.

Put some potting soil in the clay
pot. Next, make a little hole in the dirt.
~~Plant a seed.~~ Drop a flower seed into the hole Cover it up with dirt. Now
put the pot near a sunny window. Then
give the seed a little water every day.
Soon, a tiny, green plant will grow. Be
sure it gets sunlight and water. A pretty
flower will bloum.

Revise ▶ **Improve your ideas.**

1. Read your first draft to yourself and a partner.
2. Listen to what your partner says about your ideas.
3. Make any needed changes.

Revising ▶ Improving Your Organization

When you revise for organization, you make sure your ideas are in the correct order and easy to follow.

Here's what Maria did to put her writing in the best order for improved organization.

Organization

Review — Maria reviewed her first draft for organization. She asked herself two questions:

1. Did I put the steps in the right order?
2. Did I use time-order words to connect the steps?

Ask — Maria also asked a classmate to check her essay for organization.

Make — Then she made the needed changes.

I added two time-order words to make the steps easier to follow.

Maria's Revising

I can teach you how to grow a
flower. you need a ^clay pot, some potting soil,
and a flower seed. you also need water
and sunlight.
    ^First, Put some potting soil in the clay
pot. Next, make a little hole in the dirt.
^Plant a seed. Drop a flower seed into the hole Cover it up with dirt. Now
put the pot near a sunny window. Then
give the seed a little water every day.
Soon, a tiny, green plant will grow. Be
sure it gets sunlight and water. ^Finally, A pretty
flower will bloum.

Revise ▶ **Improve your organization.**

1. Review your first draft for organization.
2. Ask a classmate to check your writing
   for organization.
3. Make any needed changes.

Revising ▶ Improving Your Voice

When you revise for voice, you make sure that you sound confident and excited about your topic. If you know a lot about your topic, your writing should have voice.

Here's what Maria did to check her writing for voice.

Read Maria reread her first draft. She asked herself two questions:

> 1. Do I sound confident in every part?
> 2. Do I sound excited about the activity?

Ask Maria also asked her teacher to check her essay for voice.

Make Then she made any needed changes.

> I added a sentence that helps me sound more confident.

Maria's Revising

I can teach you how to grow a

flower. you need a ^clay pot, some potting soil,

and a flower seed. you also need water

and sunlight. ^Then just follow these steps.

^First, ^Put some potting soil in the clay

pot. Next, make a little hole in the dirt.

^Plant a seed. ^Drop a flower seed into the hole Cover it up with dirt. Now

put the pot near a sunny window. Then

give the seed a little water every day.

Soon, a tiny, green plant will grow. Be

sure it gets sunlight and water. ^Finally, A pretty

flower will bloum.

Revise ▶ **Improve your voice.**

1. Reread your first draft to be sure that you sound confident and excited about your topic.

2. Ask your teacher to check your writing for voice.

3. Make any needed changes.

Editing ▶ Checking Your Conventions

After revising your first draft, it's time to check it for capitalization, punctuation, and spelling.

Conventions

These are the things that Maria did to edit her writing for conventions.

Check Maria checked for conventions using the checklist below as a guide.

Ask She also asked a classmate to check her essay for conventions.

Mark Then Maria marked her errors and corrected them. You can see her changes on the next page.

Did you check?

✔ 1. Did you capitalize names and the first word of each sentence?

✔ 2. Did you use punctuation at the end of each sentence?

✔ 3. Did you spell your words correctly?

Maria's Editing

I can teach you how to grow a flower.
you need a clay pot, some potting soil,
and a flower seed. you also need water
and sunlight. Then just follow these steps.

First, put some potting soil in the
clay pot. Next, make a little hole in the
dirt. Drop a flower seed into the hole.
Cover it up with dirt. Now put the pot
near a sunny window. Then give the seed
a little water every day. Soon, a tiny,
green plant will grow. Be sure it gets
sunlight and water. Finally, a pretty
flower will bloom (bloum).

Edit ▶ Check for conventions.

1. Check your revised essay for conventions.
2. Ask a partner to check for conventions, too.
3. Mark any errors and correct them.

Publishing ▶ Sharing Your Essay

Maria's How-To Essay

How to Grow a Flower

    I can teach you how to grow a flower. You need a clay pot, some potting soil, and a flower seed. You also need water and sunlight. Then just follow these steps.

    First, put some potting soil in the clay pot. Next, make a little hole in the dirt. Drop a flower seed into the hole. Cover it up with dirt. Now put the pot near a sunny window. Then give the seed a little water every day. Soon, a tiny, green plant will grow. Be sure it gets sunlight and water. Finally, a pretty flower will bloom.

    I like growing flowers because they are pretty. It is fun to watch them grow. When they bloom, I pick them for my mom.

Publish ▶ **Share your essay.**

Reflecting on Your Writing

After you finish your how-to essay, take some time to think about it. Then fill in a sheet like this about your essay.

Thinking About Your Writing

Name: _Maria_

Title: _How to Grow a Flower_

1. The best thing about my essay is

   that I put the steps in the

   right order.

2. The main thing I learned while writing my essay is _that it is important to_

   sound confident.

Using a Rubric

The rubric on these pages can help you rate your writing.

Great!

6 5 4

Ideas

6 The topic and details are well developed.	5 The topic is clear and uses many details.	4 The details tell about the topic.

Organization

6 All parts of the essay are strong.	5 The beginning, middle, and ending work well.	4 The parts of the essay are in order.

Voice

6 The confident voice helps make the essay memorable.	5 The voice sounds confident and interesting.	4 For the most part, the voice is confident and interesting.

Conventions

6 Conventions are used well.	5 Most conventions are correct.	4 There are a few errors.

Literature Connections: You can find expository writing in *Basket Weaving* by Becky Manfredini.

Keep Trying!

3   **2**   **1**

| 3 More details are needed. | 2 Details that don't fit the topic confuse the reader. | 1 The topic is not clear. |

| 3 Some parts are not in order. | 2 All parts of the essay run together. | 1 The order of information is confusing. |

| 3 Sometimes, the voice sounds confident. | 2 For the most part, the voice of the writing is unclear. | 1 The writing lacks voice. |

| 3 Errors may confuse the reader. | 2 Errors make the essay hard to understand. | 1 Help is needed to make corrections. |

Writing
Across the Curriculum

Science: An Animal Report

In her science class, Kelli wrote an expository essay about warthogs.

Warthogs

Beginning

Warthogs look like hairy pigs. They have tusks, long legs, and warts on their faces. Sometimes, birds sit on their backs. The birds eat bugs that live on the warthog.

Middle

What do you think warthogs eat? They eat grass and seeds. They also like berries, bark, and roots. Once in a while, warthogs even eat bugs and dead animals!

Ending

Warthogs live in Africa. They like to hide in aardvark tunnels. When predators come along, warthogs charge at them with their sharp tusks. Stay away from warthogs!

Writing Tips

Before You Write

Gathering Questions

Think of an animal.

Read about the animal.

Answer three questions about it.

Animal: _____

1. What does it look like?
2. What does it eat?
3. Where does it live?

During Your Writing

Name the animal and **tell** what it looks like in the beginning.

Explain what it eats in the middle.

Describe where it lives in the ending.

After You Have Written

Revise your writing so that every part is clear.

Check for capitalization, punctuation, and spelling errors.

Make a neat final copy.

Practical Writing: An Invitation

In class, Paulo wrote an invitation. He asked his aunt to come to a special event at his school.

Date

November 4, 2011

Greeting

Dear Aunt Rosa,

Body
Sentences

Our class is having a play to celebrate Thanksgiving. It will be in Room 44 on November 24. The play begins at two o'clock. I will be a Pilgrim in the play. We will show how the Pilgrims made their Thanksgiving dinner. Let me know if you can come.

Closing

Love,

Signature

Paulo

Writing Tips

5 W's Chart

Before You Write

Think of a special event.

Answer the 5 W questions about the event.

Who is holding the event?
What is the event?
When and **where** will it be?
Why should people attend?

Who?	
What?	
When?	
Where?	
Why?	

During Your Writing

Begin with the date and the greeting.
Answer the 5 W's in the body sentences.
Use a closing like **Love** or **Your friend** and sign your name.

After You Have Written

Change any parts that could be improved.
Correct any errors and make a neat copy.

Writing for Assessment

On most writing tests, you will read a prompt and write a paragraph about it.

Writing Prompt

Think of a game you like to play. Write a paragraph that explains how to play it. Tell why you like the game.

Think Yoshi thought about games he has played.

List He listed some and circled the one he wanted to write about.

Draw Then Yoshi drew a picture to help him write his paragraph.

List of Ideas

Games I like to play

  kickball

  (the snail)

  baseball

Yoshi's Drawing

Yoshi's How-To Paragraph

The topic sentence names the game.

The body sentences tell how to play the game.

The closing sentence gives a final idea.

Learn to Play Snail

I know a game called snail. First, you draw a really big snail on the sidewalk. Give the snail an open mouth and a huge stomach. Then put a small stone into the snail's mouth. Hop on one foot and try to kick the stone into the stomach and back to the mouth. If you do it, you get one point. If you touch a line, you don't get a point. Each player takes five turns. The player with the most points wins. I love this game because it is fun to hop.

practice

1. Make a list of games you play.
2. Choose your topic and draw a picture (if you wish).
3. Write your paragraph.

Persuasive Writing

Writing Focus

- Persuasive Paragraph
- Persuasive Letter
- Across the Curriculum
- Writing for Assessment

Academic Vocabulary

Work with a partner. Read the meanings and share answers to the questions.

1. When you persuade someone, you get him or her to believe or act a certain way.
   When might you persuade someone?

2. An opinion is how you feel about something.
   What is your opinion about today's weather?

3. If a fact supports a statement, it helps show that the statement is true.
   What facts might support this statement: *We need to save water?*

Healthy kids are happy kids! That is one child's **opinion,** or personal feeling. When you state an opinion, you let others know how you feel about a topic.

In persuasive writing, you try to get the reader to accept your opinion. If you are really persuasive, you may even be able to convince the reader to take action!

Literature Connections: You can find persuasive language in *Saving Money* by Mary Firestone.

Writing a
Persuasive
Paragraph

Eva's class was discussing healthy living. She noticed how tired her friend Polly looked. It gave her an idea for a persuasive paragraph. Eva decided to write a paragraph to persuade her classmates to get more sleep.

In this chapter, you will write a paragraph to persuade your classmates to make a healthy choice.

Eva's Persuasive Paragraph

Go to Sleep!

Topic Sentence

You should get ten hours of sleep each night. Sleep helps you stay healthy and happy. It gives

Body Sentences

your body and brain a rest from a hard day. Best of all, sleep gives you energy to do fun things, like jumping rope and riding bikes. So every night,

Closing Sentence

you should get plenty of sleep!

- The **topic sentence** states your opinion.
- The **body sentences** give two or three reasons for your opinion.
- The **closing sentence** tells the reader what action to take.

Prewriting ▶ Choosing Your Topic

To plan a persuasive paragraph, you first must select a strong topic.

This is what Eva did to find a topic for her paragraph. Eva thought about her class discussion. She then made a cluster of topic ideas and starred the strongest topic.

Topic Cluster

Prewrite ▶ **Choose your topic.**

1. Think about what you have learned about healthy living.
2. Make a cluster of topic ideas. Star the one you want to write about.

Stating Your Opinion

You should then state your opinion or main feeling about your topic. This statement will be your topic sentence.

This is what Eva did to write her topic sentence. Eva thought about her feelings about her topic. Then she wrote her topic sentence by beginning with the words *you should.*

Topic Sentence

You should get ten hours of sleep each night.

Beginning with the words **you should** is a good way to start.

Prewrite ▶ **State your opinion.**

1. Think about the feelings you have about the topic you have chosen.
2. Write your topic sentence by beginning with the words *you should.*

Prewriting ▶ Gathering Details

Next, you should gather details to support your opinion.

This is what Eva did to gather details. She reviewed her topic sentence. Then Eva listed reasons for her opinion. She chose the most important reason and circled it.

Eva's Topic Sentence

You should get ten hours of sleep each night.

List of Reasons

Sleep helps you to be healthy and happy.

Sleep lets your body and brain rest.

⟨Sleep gives you more energy.⟩

Prewrite ▶ Gather details.

1. List the reasons for your opinion.
2. Choose the most important reason and circle it.

Writing ▶ **Writing Your First Draft**

Your persuasive paragraph must contain a topic sentence, body sentences, and a closing sentence.

This is what Eva did to write the first draft of her persuasive paragraph. Eva reviewed her topic sentence (opinion statement) and reasons list. Then Eva wrote her paragraph. She followed these steps.

1. She started with her topic sentence or opinion statement.
2. Next, Eva stated her reasons in the body sentences.
3. She closed her paragraph by telling the reader to take action.

State your most important reason last.

Write ▶ **Write your first draft.**

1. Review your opinion statement and reasons list.
2. Write your paragraph following Eva's three steps.

Revising ▶ Improving Your Writing

After finishing your first draft, it's time to improve your paragraph.

Eva revised her paragraph. First, she reviewed her opinion statement and three supporting reasons. Next, Eva checked that she had stated the most important reason last. Finally, she made any needed changes.

Be sure that you sound convincing in your paragraph.

Revise ▶ **Improve your writing.**

1. Review your opinion statement and reasons.
2. Check that your most important reason is last.
3. Make any needed changes to improve your paragraph.

Editing ▶ Checking for Conventions

The next important step is to check the conventions in your revised paragraph.

This is what Eva did to edit her revised paragraph. First, she reviewed her paragraph for conventions using the checklist below. After checking, Eva corrected any errors.

Did you check?

✓ 1. Did you capitalize names and the first word of each sentence?

✓ 2. Did you use punctuation at the end of each sentence?

✓ 3. Did you spell your words correctly?

Edit ▶ **Check for conventions.**

1. Review your revised paragraph for conventions. Use the checklist above as a guide.

2. Correct any errors that you find.

Writing a
Persuasive
Letter

"I eat too much junk food!" That was Mary's opinion about her diet. She wondered if she could do anything about it. She decided to write a persuasive letter to her mom and dad.

In this chapter, you will learn how to write a persuasive letter. In your letter, you will tell about one way to stay healthy.

Goals for Writing

The traits below will help you write your letter. Read them carefully before you get started.

Your goal is to . . .

Ideas

Write an opinion sentence and give reasons that support it.

Organization

Put the parts of your letter in the correct order.

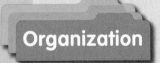

Voice

Sound serious and polite in your letter.

Conventions

Check your capitalization, punctuation, and spelling.

Mary's Persuasive Letter

Date

January 12, 2012

Greeting

Dear Mom and Dad,

We should remember to eat snacks that are healthy. At school, I tasted broccoli and soy nuts. I even tried yogurt. Guess what? They taste good!

Body

Vegetables, fruits, grains, and dairy foods are good for us. They can help us think, work, and play better. Best of all, they can keep us healthy.

I think we all should eat many more healthy snacks. Please buy some extra ones the next time you go shopping.

Closing

Love,

Signature

Mary

Parts of a Letter

A friendly letter has five parts.

Date
: The date tells when you wrote the letter.

Greeting
: The greeting is a polite way of saying, "Hi."

Body
: The body is the main part of the letter.

Closing
: The closing is a polite way of saying, "Good-bye."

Signature
: The signature is the name of the writer at the end of the letter.

After You Read

1. **Ideas** What is Mary's opinion? What does she want her parents to do?

2. **Organization** What closing does Mary use in her letter?

3. **Voice** Do you think Mary was polite in her letter? Why or why not?

Prewriting ▶ **Forming an Opinion**

When planning for a persuasive letter, first form an opinion about the topic of your choice.

Here is what Conall did to get started.

Make Conall made a table diagram of ideas, and he starred the best topic.

Write Next, Conall wrote his opinion statement about his topic.

Table Diagram

Staying Healthy		
drink water	eat breakfast	*wash your hands

Write your own opinion statement by starting with **you should**.

<u>You should</u> **remember to wash your hands.**

Prewrite ▶ **Form an opinion.**

1. Make a table diagram to list your topics.
2. Write an opinion statement about your topic.

Gathering Details

Next, list reasons to support your opinion and decide who you could write your letter to.

Here's what Conall did to gather details for his letter.

List He listed reasons to support his opinion and circled the most important one.

Pick Then Conall picked someone to write to.

List of Reasons

Opinion:
You should remember to wash your hands.
Reasons:
To keep your food safe
To stop germs from spreading
To keep you from getting sick

Prewrite ▶ **Gather details.**

1. List reasons to support your opinion and circle the most important one.
2. Pick someone to write to.

Writing ▶ Creating Your Letter

When you write your letter, be sure to include the five main parts. (See page 139.) Then concentrate on writing the body paragraphs.

This is what Conall did to write the body paragraphs for his persuasive letter.

I used these guidelines to write my first draft.

Guidelines

1. Start the **beginning paragraph** with your opinion. Then add one or two details about the topic.

2. Explain your reasons in the **middle paragraph.** Put your most important reason last.

3. In the **ending paragraph**, add an interesting detail and ask the reader to do something.

Conall's first draft contains three paragraphs.

Conall's First Draft

Dear Mrs. Martin's Class,

Hi. You should remember to wash your hands. Germs live on your skin. they even hid.

Wash your hands. It stops germs from spreading. Best of all, it keeps you from getting sick. Washing hands keeps your food safer, too.

Come on! Make school a healthyr place. Wash your hands!

Sincerely,
Conall

Write ▶ **Create your letter.**

1. Follow the letter form on page 138.
2. Write your body paragraphs.

Revising ▶ Improving Your Ideas

When you review your letter, pay careful attention to your ideas. Change any of them that could be clearer or more interesting.

Here's what Conall did to revise his letter for ideas.

Ideas

Review   Conall reviewed his letter to make sure that his details were clear and interesting.

Ask   He also asked a classmate to read his first draft.

Change   Conall then changed his writing to make it clearer.

I added two new details. It made my letter clearer and more interesting.

Conall's Revising

Dear Mrs. Martin's Class,

    Hi. You should remember to wash your hands. Germs live on your skin. they even hid.

    Scrub
    with soap and water
    Wash your hands. It stops germs from spreading. Best of all, it keeps you from getting sick. Washing hands keeps your food safer, too.

         You can
    Come on! Make school a healthyr
Send those germs down the drain.
place. Wash your hands!

           Sincerely,

           Conall

Revise ▶ Improve your ideas.

1. Review your first draft and have a classmate read it, too.
2. Change any ideas that could be clearer.

Revising ▶ Improving Your Organization

When revising, pay careful attention to the order of your ideas. Move any of them that seem out of place.

Here's what Conall did to revise his body paragraphs for organization.

Organization

Review   Conall made sure that his opinion was stated in the beginning and that his supporting reasons were in the best order.

Ask   Conall asked his teacher to check his organization.

Reorder   He then moved any ideas that seemed out of place.

I moved my most important reason last.

Conall's Revising

Dear Mrs. Martin's Class,

Hi. You should remember to wash your hands. Germs live on your skin. they even hid.

Scrub ~~Wash~~ your hands *with soap and water*. It stops germs from spreading. ~~Best of all, it keeps you from getting sick.~~ Washing hands keeps your food safer, too. ↓

Come on! *You can* Make school a healthyr place. *Send those germs down the drain.* Wash your hands!

Sincerely,
Conall

Revise ► Improve your organization.

1. Review your first draft for organization and have a teacher read it, too.
2. Reorder any ideas that seem out of place.

Revising ▶ Improving Your Voice

When revising, listen to the voice that you use. Change or cut any ideas that do not sound polite or serious enough for a persuasive letter.

Here's what Conall did to revise his letter for voice.

Read First, Conall read his first draft to make sure that all of his ideas were polite and serious.

Listen Then he listened while a classmate read the letter out loud.

Change He changed or cut any ideas that did not have the right voice.

I cut two ideas that did not sound serious or polite enough.

Conall's Revising

Dear Mrs. Martin's Class,

~~Hi!~~ You should remember to wash your hands. Germs live on your skin. they even hid.

Scrub ~~Wash~~ *with soap and water* your hands. It stops germs from spreading. ~~Best of all, it keeps you from getting sick.~~ Washing hands keeps your food safer, too.

~~Come on!~~ *You can* Make school a healthyr place. *Send those germs down the drain.* Wash your hands!

Sincerely,

Conall

Revise ▶ **Improve your voice.**

1. Read your first draft and listen while a classmate reads it out loud to you.
2. Change or cut any ideas as needed.

Editing ▶ Checking Your Conventions

When you edit, you check your writing for conventions.

This is how Conall edited his persuasive letter.

Conventions

Review Conall reviewed his letter to make sure it included the five main parts. (See page 138.)

Check He also checked his letter for any errors. He used the checklist below as a guide.

Correct Then Conall marked his errors and corrected them.

I used this checklist to edit my writing.

Did you check?

✔ 1. Did you capitalize names and the first word of each sentence?

✔ 2. Did you use punctuation at the end of each sentence?

✔ 3. Did you spell your words correctly?

Conall's Editing

January 20, 2011

Dear Mrs. Martin's Class,

You should remember to wash
your hands. Germs live on your skin. ~~they~~ They
even ~~hid~~ hide.

Scrub your hands with water. It stops germs from spreading.
Washing hands keeps your food safer,
too. Best of all, it keeps you from
getting sick.

You can make school a ~~healthyr~~ healthier
place. Send those germs down the drain.
Wash your hands!

Sincerely,

Conall

Edit ▶ **Check for conventions.**

1. Check capitalization, punctuation, and spelling.
2. Check, mark, and correct any errors.

Publishing ▶ Sharing Your Letter

When you publish your writing, you share the final copy. There are many different ways to publish. (See page 33.)

Here's what Conall did to publish his letter.

Write Conall wrote a neat final copy of his letter. He included all of his revising and editing changes.

Read Then he read this copy to be sure it was neat and free of mistakes.

I shared my letter and then added it to my writing portfolio.

Conall's Persuasive Letter

January 20, 2011

Dear Mrs. Martin's Class,

You should remember to wash your hands. Germs live on our skin. They even hide.

Scrub your hands with soap and water. It stops germs from spreading. Washing hands keeps your food safer, too. Best of all, it keeps you from getting sick.

You can make school a healthier place. Send those germs down the drain. Wash your hands!

Sincerely,
Conall

Publish ▶ **Share your letter.**

1. Write a neat copy of your letter.
2. Read the final copy before you share it.

Sending Your Letter

To send your letter, fold it neatly into three parts. Then put it into an envelope.

> Remember: The U.S. Postal Service asks that you use all capital letters and no punctuation when addressing your envelope.

Addressing Your Envelope

1. Write your name and address in the upper left corner.
2. In the middle of the envelope, write the name and address of the person who will get your letter.
3. Place a stamp in the upper right corner.

CONALL RIOS
879 64TH AVENUE
MILTON MA 02186

USA ¢

MRS MARTIN
ROBERT FROST SCHOOL
96 ELM STREET
MILTON MA 02186

Reflecting on Your Writing

Take a few minutes to think about your writing. Complete the two sentences below.

Thinking About Your Writing

Name: _Conall Rios_

Title: _Friendly Letter_

1. The best thing about my letter is

   the part about sending germs right

   down the drain!

2. The main thing I learned while writing

   my letter is _that it's important to have_

   good reasons for your opinion.

Using a Rubric

The rubric on these pages can help you rate your writing.

Great!

6   5   4

Ideas
6 The opinion and reasons are strong.
5 Reasons support a strong opinion.
4 An opinion is given with some reasons.

Organization
6 All parts of the letter work well.
5 The letter is written in logical order.
4 Most of the letter is in order.

Voice
6 The voice is serious, polite, and convincing.
5 The voice sounds serious and polite.
4 In most parts, the voice sounds serious and polite.

Conventions
6 Conventions are used well.
5 Conventions are correct.
4 There are a few errors.

Literature Connections: You can find persuasive language in the article *No Helmet? Pay up!*

Keep Trying!

3 | **2** | **1**

3 More reasons need to support the opinion.	**2** The writing needs to focus on one opinion.	**1** The opinion of the writer is unclear.
3 Some parts need to be put in order.	**2** All parts of the letter run together.	**1** The essay needs to be organized.
3 Sometimes, the voice is not serious or polite enough.	**2** The voice of the writer is not serious or polite.	**1** The writing lacks voice.
3 Errors confuse the reader.	**2** Errors make the essay hard to read.	**1** Help is needed to make corrections.

Writing
Across the Curriculum
Science: Endangered Animal Paragraph

For science, Juanita wrote a persuasive paragraph about an endangered animal.

Save the Tigers

Topic Sentence

> Our class should help save the tigers. We could have a penny drive

Body Sentences

> and give the pennies to the Wild Tiger Fund. Then people could use the money to save the grasslands where tigers live. We need to take action. It would be sad to see these big, beautiful cats disappear. The tigers really need

Closing Sentence

> us. Please say yes to a penny drive!

Writing Tips

Before You Write

Think of a cause that you have discussed in class.

Form an opinion statement about one of these causes.

Use a cluster to gather supporting reasons.

Cluster

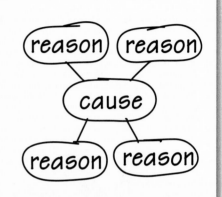

During Your Writing

State your opinion in the topic sentence.

Give reasons for supporting this cause in the body sentences.

Ask your reader to take action in the closing sentence.

After You Have Written

Be sure you included important reasons.

Check your capitalization, punctuation, and spelling.

Social Studies: Flier for an Event

Henry made a flier for social studies. He invited his family to attend a special program in his classroom.

Meet the Pioneers!

Play their games. Sample their foods. Learn about log cabins. Sing pioneer songs and see a covered wagon.

Who: Students in Mrs. Chua's Class
What: Present an Evening with the Pioneers
When: 6:30 P.M. on Friday, February 20
Where: Room 20, Bain Elementary School

We will have lots of fun!
PLEASE COME!

Writing Tips

Before You Write

Think of an event that your class will or could present.
Gather details in a 5 W's chart.

5 W's Chart

Who?	
What?	
When?	
Where?	
Why?	

During Your Writing

Name the event in the title of the flier.
Tell what will happen at the event in a short paragraph.
List who, what, when, and where facts.
Add a sentence to tell why people should attend.

After You Have Written

Be sure you included the main facts.
Check your capitalization, punctuation, and spelling.
Make a neat final copy of your flier.

Writing for Assessment

You may be asked to write a persuasive paragraph for a writing assessment.

Writing Prompt

Imagine that your class can take a field trip to any place you have studied. Choose a place. In one paragraph, persuade your class to go there.

Think   Lila thought about places to go.

Choose   She chose to write about a very special place, Washington, D.C.

List   Then she listed reasons to support her choice. She circled the most important reason.

List of Reasons

1. We could go to the White House.
2. We might meet the president.
3. We could visit the National Zoo.

Lila's Persuasive Paragraph

A Capital Idea

<table>
<tr>
<td>

The **topic sentence** names the place.

</td>
<td>

    Our class should go to Washington, D.C. It is an exciting city with many things to see and do. First, we'll visit the National Zoo.

</td>
</tr>
<tr>
<td>

The **body sentences** explain the field trip.

</td>
<td>

Next, we could see the White House where many presidents have lived. Best of all, we might even meet the president.

</td>
</tr>
<tr>
<td>

The **closing sentences** give a call to action.

</td>
<td>

We should plan a field trip to Washington, D.C. Let's do it!

</td>
</tr>
</table>

practice

1. Think of places you have studied.
2. Choose one you want your class to visit.
3. List reasons like the ones on page 162.
4. Write your persuasive paragraph.

www.hmheducation.com/writesource

Responding to Literature

Writing Focus

- Response Paragraph
- Reviewing a Fiction and a Nonfiction Book
- Comparing Fiction Books
- Responding to a Poem
- Writing for Assessment

Academic Vocabulary

Work with a partner. Read the meanings and share your answers.

1. When you read literature, you read stories, books, or poems.
   What kinds of literature do you like?

2. When you compare, you decide how two things are alike.
   Compare yourself and your partner.

3. A guide is something that shows the way.
   How can a guide help you build something?

Don't keep a good book to yourself. Tell your friends about it! Talking about books can be fun. You can also share your ideas by writing about the books you've read.

In this section, you will learn how to write about literature. Writing about the stories and poems that you read really helps you think about them—and understand them better.

Writing a
Response
Paragraph

After Mark read a story, he decided he was like one of the characters. He wrote about this idea in a response paragraph.

In this chapter, you will respond to a story in the same way.

Mark's Response Paragraph

By Myself

Topic Sentence

  I am like Frog in the book Days with Frog and Toad by Arnold Lobel. In the story, Frog writes Toad a note. It says, "I went out, and I want to be alone." Toad

Body Sentences

thinks Frog does not want to be his friend, but Frog just wants to be by himself. Sometimes I like to be alone like Frog. Maybe I will write

Closing Sentence

my friends a note like that. I hope they will understand how I feel.

- The **topic sentence** names the character, the book, and the author.
- The **body sentences** tell how the writer is like the character.
- The **closing sentence** shares one last idea.

Prewriting ▶ Planning Your Writing

After you select a story to write about, gather details for your response paragraph.

Mark finished the sentence starters below to gather details about the story he read.

Sentence Starters

1. The title of this book is __Days with Frog and Toad__

2. The author is __Arnold Lobel__

3. I am like __Frog__ because __sometimes I like to be alone.__

4. The part of the story that shows this is __when Frog writes to Toad.__

Prewrite ▶ **Gather your details.**

1. Choose a book you would like to write about.
2. Then finish the sentence starters above on your own paper.

Writing ▶ Writing Your First Draft

Use the details you have gathered to write your paragraph. Include a topic sentence, body sentences, and a closing sentence.

> Mark wrote his first draft using ideas from the sentence starters on page 168.

Write ▶ **Create your paragraph.**

1. Write your topic sentence.

I am like _____ (character's name) _____
in the book _____ (book's title) _____
by _____ (name of author) _____.

2. Write body sentences. Show how you are like the character. Use one example from the story.
3. End with a closing sentence. Share one last idea about your topic.

Revising ▶ Improving Your Writing

Review your first draft to make sure the ideas are clear and easy to follow. Then change any parts as needed.

Mark carefully reviewed his first draft using the checklist below as a guide. Then he changed parts that could be improved.

Did you review?

✓ 1. Did you name the book and author?

✓ 2. Did you tell how you are like one of the characters?

✓ 3. Did you use an example from the story to show this?

✓ 4. Did you put your ideas in order so they make sense?

Revise ▶ **Improve your writing.**

1. Review your first draft using the checklist above as a guide.
2. Change parts that could be improved.

Editing ▶ Checking Your Conventions

When you edit your paragraph, you check it for conventions. It's important that you use correct capitalization, punctuation, and spelling.

Mark edited his writing using the checklist as a guide. He also asked a classmate to check his writing.

Did you check?

✔ 1. Did you indent the first line of your paragraph?

✔ 2. Did you underline the book's title?

✔ 3. Did you capitalize names and the first word in each sentence?

✔ 4. Did you use a punctuation mark after each sentence?

✔ 5. Did you check your spelling?

Edit ▶ Check for conventions.

1. Edit your writing using the checklist above as a guide.
2. Also ask a classmate to check your paragraph for conventions.

Reviewing a
Fiction Book

A fiction (make-believe) book helps you imagine another world. Stacy, who lives in a big city, enjoyed reading *All the Places to Love*. The book helped her imagine living in the country. She wrote a review about the story.

In this chapter, you will write a review about a fiction book you have read.

Stacy's Book Review

Special Places

Beginning

 All the Places to Love was written by Patricia MacLachlan. In the story, a boy named Eli lives on a farm. He wants to share his special places with his new baby sister.

Middle

 My favorite part is when Baby Sylvie is born. Eli thinks about showing her the marsh. It is his favorite place. A turtle lives there, and baby ducklings swim in the water.

Ending

 You should read this book. The words sound like a poem, and the pictures are pretty. If you live in the city, Eli will share his farm with you.

After You Read

1. **Ideas** What is the main idea of the book?
2. **Organization** What does the middle part of the review tell about?

Prewriting ▶ Selecting a Topic

To get started, think of your favorite fiction books. Then choose one to be the topic of your review.

Here's how Zola selected a book for her review.

Build   Zola built a question grid about her two favorite fiction books and circled one book to review.

Question Grid

What is the title?	Who is the author?	Why do I like the book?
Cloudy with a Chance of Meatballs	Judi Barrett	It is very funny.
Nate the Great	Marjorie Weinman Sharmat and Mitchell Sharmat	I like mysteries.

Prewrite ▶ **Select a topic.**

1. Fill in a question grid about your two favorite books.
2. Circle the book you want to write about.

Gathering Details

After selecting a favorite book, you need to gather details before you can write about it.

Here's what Zola did to gather details for her book review.

Fill in   Zola filled in a 5 W's chart with important details from the book.

5 W's Chart

Who?	Nate, his dog Sludge, and Duncan were there.
What?	Duncan lost his joke book. Nate helped him find it.
When?	The story happened yesterday.
Where?	The story happened in San Francisco.
Why?	Duncan made a mess at the Pancake House.

Prewrite ▶ **Gather details.**

Fill in a 5 W's chart like the one above about your book.

Writing ▶ Beginning Your Review

In your beginning paragraph, name the book and the author. Also tell what the book is about.

This is how Zola began.

Write   Zola checked her 5 W's chart for details and wrote her beginning paragraph.

Zola's Beginning Paragraph

> <u>Nate the Great, San Francisco Detective</u> was written by Marjorie Weinman Sharmat and Mitchell Sharmat. In this story, Nate goes to San Francisco. He helps a boy named Duncan look for a lost book. Nate is a great detective because he finds lots of clues.

Write ▶ Begin your review.

Write your beginning using your 5 W's chart.

Telling Just Enough

In Zola's beginning paragraph, she did not give away any of the surprises or the story's ending. She told just enough details to make her friends want to read the book for themselves.

practice

Here is another beginning paragraph about Zola's book. Which two sentences give away surprises? Tell why these sentences should be left out.

(1) Nate the Great, San Francisco Detective was written by Marjorie Weinman Sharmat and Mitchell Sharmat. **(2)** The story happens in San Francisco. **(3)** Nate, the detective, helps a boy named Duncan look for a lost book. **(4)** It is in the bookstore on the wrong shelf. **(5)** In the end, the mystery is solved.

Writing ▶ Developing the Middle

The middle paragraph of your review should tell about your favorite part of the book.

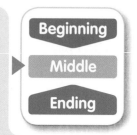

Here's what Zola did to write the middle paragraph of her review.

Think   Zola thought about her favorite part of the book.

Write   Then she wrote a paragraph about this part. She shared the details in time order.

Zola's Middle Paragraph

> The best part is when Nate digs for clues in a messy bag. He finds dirty napkins, cold pancakes, and a small tub of butter. It gets worse. Sticky maple syrup is on everything.

Write   ▶ **Develop the middle.**

Write a paragraph about your favorite part of the book.

Completing the Ending

The ending paragraph of your review should tell why you think your classmates will enjoy the book.

Here's how Zola wrote her ending.

Think Zola thought about why she liked the book.

Decide She decided her classmates would like it for the same reason.

Write Then Zola wrote her ending paragraph.

Zola's Ending Paragraph

> Do you wish you were a detective? You can be one when you read <u>Nate the Great, San Francisco Detective.</u> It is fun trying to solve the mystery. See if you can figure it out before Nate does.

Write ▶ **Complete the ending.**

Write your ending paragraph. Tell why your classmates should read the book.

Revising ▶ Improving Your Writing

You should review your first draft and revise or change any ideas that could be clearer.

Here's what Zola did to revise her first draft.

Review Zola reviewed her writing using the checklist below as a guide.

Identify She identified any parts that could be clearer.

Change Then Zola changed the parts that needed work.

Did you review?

✔ 1. Did you name the book and its author?

✔ 2. Did you share your favorite part?

✔ 3. Did you include just enough details without spoiling the ending?

Revise ▶ **Improve your writing.**

1. Review your first draft using the checklist above.
2. Change any parts that need work.

Editing ▶ Checking for Conventions

After revising your book review, you should check it for capitalization, punctuation, and spelling.

This is what Zola did to edit her writing.

Use   Zola used the questions below as an editing guide.

Mark   She marked any convention errors.

Correct   Then Zola corrected the errors.

Did you check?

✓ 1. Did you capitalize names and the first word in each sentence?

✓ 2. Did you use correct punctuation after each sentence?

✓ 3. Did you underline the book's title?

✓ 4. Did you check your spelling?

Edit ▶ **Check for conventions.**

Edit your writing using the questions above as a guide.

Publishing ▶ Sharing Your Review

Zola's Book Review

The Great Nate

    Nate the Great, San Francisco Detective
was written by Marjorie Weinman Sharmat
and Mitchell Sharmat. In this story, Nate
goes to San Francisco. He helps a boy named
Duncan look for a lost book. Nate is a great
detective because he finds lots of clues.
    The best part is when Nate digs for
clues in a messy bag. He finds dirty napkins,
cold pancakes, and a small tub of butter.
It gets worse. Sticky maple syrup is on
everything!
    Do you wish you were a detective? You
can be one when you read Nate the Great,
San Francisco Detective. It is fun trying to
solve the mystery. See if you can figure it
out before Nate does.

Publish ▶ **Share a neat final copy of
your review.**

Reflecting on Your Writing

After you finish your review, take some time to think about it. Then fill in a chart like this about your review.

Thinking About Your Writing

Name: _Zola_

Title: _The Great Nate_

1. The best part about my review is

   the ending. My question makes the

   reader think.

2. The main thing I learned while writing

   my review is _that it's really important_

   not to give the whole story away.

Reviewing a
Nonfiction Book

Nonfiction books give true facts about real people, places, and things. Lee wrote a review about the nonfiction book *Cactus Hotel*. Read his review and then learn how to write one of your own.

Lee's Book Review

A Desert Home

Beginning

   Cactus Hotel is a book by Brenda Z. Guiberson. It tells about the life of a saguaro cactus. This giant plant grows in the desert.

Middle

   Here are some interesting facts from the book. When it rains, a saguaro cactus gets fat. A saguaro can live for 200 years. Birds make holes in the cactus. The holes become homes for animals.

Ending

   My favorite page shows birds, bugs, and rats living inside a saguaro cactus. When one animal moves out, another one moves in. Can you see why it is called a cactus hotel?

After You Read

1. **Ideas** What is the main idea of the book?
2. **Organization** What does the ending part tell about?

Prewriting ▶ Selecting a Topic

To get started, think of your favorite nonfiction books. Then choose one to be the topic of your review.

Here's what Debra did to select a book.

Make Debra made a chart about two of her favorite nonfiction books. (See below.)

Star Then Debra starred the book she chose.

Book Chart

Title 1	Jambo Means Hello *
Author	Muriel Feelings
Main Idea	Swahili words tell about life in Africa.
Title 2	All Pigs Are Beautiful
Author	Dick King-Smith
Main Idea	You learn all about pigs.

Prewrite ▶ **Select a topic.**

1. Make a book chart about two favorite nonfiction books.
2. Star the book that you want to review.

Gathering Details

After you choose a nonfiction book, gather details about it for your review.

This is what Debra did to gather details.

Answer   Debra answered three important questions about the book. (See below.)

Question and Answer Sheet

What is the book about?
—life in Africa
—Swahili words for each alphabet letter
What facts do I think are most interesting?
—school outdoors
—Watoto, the Swahili word for children
—children tending cattle and hauling water
Which is my favorite part? Why?
—Children dancing and playing looks like fun!

Prewrite   ▶ **Gather details.**

To gather details, answer the three questions above about your book.

Writing ▶ Your First Draft

Your review should include three parts: the beginning paragraph, the middle paragraph, and the ending paragraph. Each paragraph will answer one of the questions that you answered on page 187.

This is what Debra did to write her first draft.

Review   Debra reviewed her answers to the questions on page 187.

Write   Then she wrote her first draft.

In the **beginning** paragraph, Debra named the book's title and author. She also told what the book is about.

She shared at least three interesting facts in the **middle** paragraph.

In the **ending** paragraph, Debra told about her favorite part.

Beginning

Jambo Means Hello is a book by Muriel Feelings. It is about life in Africa. The book shows one Swahili word for each letter of the alphabet. Swahili is one of Africa's languages.

Middle

Here are some interesting facts in the book. Kids in Africa go to school outside. They have many hard chores to do. They take care of the cattle. They also haul water from the river. The Swahili word for children is Watoto.

Ending

My favorite part shows kids dancing and playing. The book says that they sing funny songs and dance with quick steps. I wish I could play with them.

Write ▶ **Write your first draft.**

1. Review your answers to the questions on page 187.
2. Write your first draft using the sample above as a guide.

Revising ▶ Improving Your Writing

Revise or change any ideas in your writing that could be clearer.

This is what Debra did to revise her writing.

Study Debra studied her first draft using the checklist below as a guide.

Change Then she changed any parts that could be clearer or more complete.

Did you review?

✔ 1. Did you name the book and its author?

✔ 2. Did you tell what the book is about?

✔ 3. Did you share at least three important facts?

✔ 4. Did you tell about your favorite part?

✔ 5. Are your ideas clear?

Revise ▶ **Improve your writing.**

1. Study your first draft using the checklist above as a guide.

2. Change any parts that could be clearer or more complete.

Editing ▶ Checking for Conventions

After revising your book review, you should check it for capitalization, punctuation, and spelling. Also have a classmate help you edit your writing.

Here's what Debra did to edit her review.

Check Debra edited her writing using the questions below as a guide.

Mark She marked any convention errors.

Correct Then Debra corrected the errors.

Did you check?

✓ 1. Did you capitalize the first word in each sentence and in names?

✓ 2. Did you use a punctuation mark after each sentence?

✓ 3. Did you underline the book's title?

✓ 4. Did you check your spelling?

Edit ▶ **Check for conventions.**

Edit your writing using the questions above as a guide.

Publishing ▶ Sharing Your Review

Debra's Response Essay

Jambo!

    <u>Jambo Means Hello</u> is a book by Muriel Feelings. It is about life in Africa. The book shows one Swahili word for each letter of the alphabet. Swahili is one of Africa's languages.

    Here are some interesting facts in the book. Kids in Africa go to school outside. They have many hard chores to do. They take care of the cattle. They also haul water from the river. The Swahili word for children is Watoto.

    My favorite page shows kids dancing and playing. The book says that they sing funny songs and dance with quick steps. I wish I could play with them.

Publish ▶ **Share a neat final copy of your review.**

Reflecting on Your Writing

After you finish your review, take some time to think about it. Then fill in a sheet like this about your review.

Thinking About Your Writing

Name: _Debra_

Title: _Jambo!_

1. The best part about my review is

   the middle. The facts are interesting.

   _____

2. The main thing I learned while writing

   my review is _how to tell what the book_

   is about in a few sentences.

Comparing
Fiction Books

Do you have a favorite author? Travis really likes Tomie dePaola. He read two great books by this author. Then he compared the two books in an essay. Read his comparison and learn how to write one of your own.

Travis's Comparison Essay

Two Long Ago Stories

Beginning   My favorite author is Tomie dePaola. I read his books The Legend of the Indian Paintbrush and Jamie O'Rourke and the Big Potato.

Middle   The books are alike because they take place long ago. Both stories are about plants. The books are different, too. In one story, the plant is a potato. In the other, it is an Indian Paintbrush. One story takes place in Ireland, and the other happens in America.

Ending   I like Jamie O'Rourke and the Big Potato best because it is funny. I like funny stories.

After You Read

1. **Ideas** How are the two books different?
2. **Organization** What information does the beginning give?

Prewriting ▶ Selecting a Topic

Think of two books by one of your favorite authors to compare. Or think of one book that you really like and find another book by the same author.

Here's what Kamika did to select two books to compare.

Name   Kamika named one of her favorite authors, Jan Brett.

Choose   Then she chose two books by this author to compare: <u>Hedgie's Surprise</u> and <u>Daisy Comes Home</u>.

You may have to use the computer catalog in your library to find one of your books.

Prewrite ▶ **Select a topic.**

1. Name your favorite author.
2. Choose two books by that author to compare. (Or think of your favorite book and another book by the same author.)

Gathering Details

Use a graphic organizer like a Venn diagram to gather details for your essay.

This is what Kamika did to gather details.

Fill in   Kamika filled in a Venn diagram with details about how the books are alike and different.

Venn Diagram

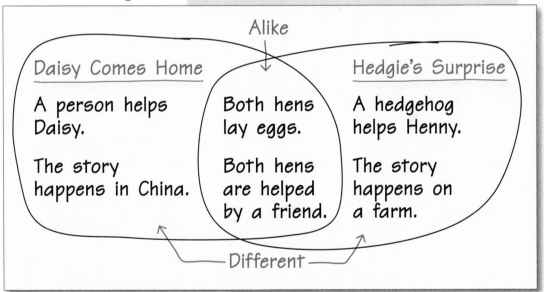

Alike

Daisy Comes Home

A person helps Daisy.

The story happens in China.

Both hens lay eggs.

Both hens are helped by a friend.

Hedgie's Surprise

A hedgehog helps Henny.

The story happens on a farm.

Different

Prewrite ▶ Gather details.

Fill in a Venn diagram to show how your books are alike and different.

Writing ▶ Writing Your First Draft

Write the beginning, middle, and ending parts of your essay.

> Here's how Kamika wrote her first draft.
>
> **Develop** Kamika used page 195 and her Venn diagram to develop her essay.

Write ▶ **Write your first draft.**

Develop the three parts of your essay.

Revising and Editing

Revise and edit your first draft to be sure that it is clear and correct.

> Here's how Kamika improved her first draft.
>
> **Change** Kamika changed any unclear parts and corrected any mistakes.

Revise ▶ **and** **Edit** ▶

Change your essay to make it clear and correct.

Publishing ▶ Sharing Your Comparison

Kamika's Response Essay

Two Hens

    I read two books by Jan Brett. They are <u>Daisy Comes Home</u> and <u>Hedgie's Surprise</u>.
    The books are alike because they are about hens that lay eggs. Both hens get help from a friend. The books are different, too. One hen is named Henny, and she lives on a farm. A hedgehog named Hedgie helps Henny. The other hen is named Daisy. She lives in a sandy yard in China. Daisy's helper is a person named Mei Mei.
    I liked <u>Daisy Comes Home</u> best because the setting is China. The pictures show an interesting, faraway place.

Publish ▶ **Share a neat final copy of your comparison.**

Responding to a
Poem

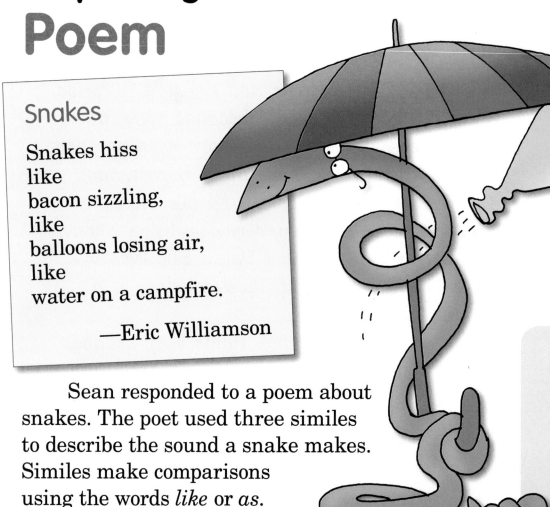

Snakes

Snakes hiss
like
bacon sizzling,
like
balloons losing air,
like
water on a campfire.

—Eric Williamson

Sean responded to a poem about
snakes. The poet used three similes
to describe the sound a snake makes.
Similes make comparisons
using the words *like* or *as*.
In this chapter, you will
learn how to respond
to a simile poem.

Sean's Response Essay

Sizzling Snakes

Beginning
  "Snakes" is a poem about sounds. It compares a snake's hissing to other sounds.

Middle
  My favorite simile is "Snakes hiss like bacon sizzling." I've heard bacon sizzling on the stove. Ssss! That's a hiss I love to hear.

Ending
  I think the poet wrote this poem because he likes using words creatively. His hissing similes are fun to read.

After You Read

1. **Ideas** What is the writer's favorite simile? Why does he like it?
2. **Organization** What does the ending part tell about?

Prewriting ▶ Choosing a Poem

Read the simile poems on this page. Think about which one you'd like to write about.

Thunder

Thunder rumbles
like
a space shuttle launch,
like
a big bass drum,
like
fireworks!

—Darin Hall

Let's Fly!

Birds fly
like
paper airplanes,
like
leaves in the winds,
like
sparks from a fire.

—Sue Ling

Stars

Stars sparkle
like
Grandfather's eyes,
like
Mother's earrings,
like
my shiny blue shoes.

—Jenna Matson

Leap Frog

Frogs leap
like
funny clowns,
like
kangaroos,
like
tummies on a
    roller coaster!

—Ty Petski

Prewrite ▶ Choose a poem.

Gathering Details

The next step is to gather details in the poem for your response.

> Here's what Mandy did to gather details.
>
> **Complete**   Mandy completed the sentence starters below to gather her details.

> Spring
>
> Flower buds wait like
> wrapped presents, like
> chicks inside eggs, like
> pages in a book.
>
> —Ellie Taylor

Sentence Starters

1. The poem "_Spring_" is about _flower buds_.

2. My favorite simile is "_Flower buds wait_ _like pages in a book_."

3. I think the poet wrote the poem because _she likes spring_.

Prewrite ▶ **Gather details.**

Copy and complete the sentence starters above.

Writing ▶ Writing Your First Draft

Develop the beginning, middle, and ending parts of your response.

> This is how Mandy wrote her response.
>
> **Develop** Mandy developed the three parts of her response using page 201 and her sentence starters as a guide.

Write ▶ **Write your first draft.**

Develop your first draft.

Revising and Editing

Be sure that your ideas are clear and correct.

> Here's how Mandy improved her response.
>
> **Change** Mandy changed any unclear parts and corrected any mistakes.

Revise ▶ and **Edit** ▶

Change your essay to make it clear and correct.

Publishing ▶ Sharing Your Response

Mandy's Response Essay

A Long Wait

"Spring" is a poem about flower buds. The buds are waiting to open. It is the season of spring.

My favorite simile is "Flower buds wait like pages in a book." I thought about that for a long time. With a book, spring can come anytime of the year. Pages in a book are always waiting for somebody to read them.

Maybe the poet wrote this poem because she is waiting for spring. She might have a flower garden in her backyard.

Publish ▶ **Make a neat final copy to share.**

Writing for Assessment

On most writing tests, you will read a prompt and write a paragraph about it.

Writing Prompt

Pretend you are one of the characters in your favorite story. Write a paragraph that tells who you are, what is happening, and how you feel.

Think Terri thought about her favorite story.

Choose She chose a character and a part of the story to write about.

Fill in Then she filled in a 5 W's chart to gather details.

Terri's Chart and Response

Who?	Pickles the dog
What?	worried about my dog license
When?	January 1
Where?	in the store
Why?	because we have no money

My name is Pickles, and I run a store with Ginger the cat. I am worried because we have no money at our store, and I can't pay for my dog license. I will ask our customers to pay their bills.

practice

1. Choose a character from your favorite story.
2. Use a 5 W's chart to gather details. Then write a response paragraph.

Creative Writing

Writing Focus

- Add-On Stories
- Creating a Play
- Writing Poems

Academic Vocabulary

Work with a partner. Read the meanings and share your answers.

1. A character is a person in a story or play. Animals or objects can also be characters. **Who are the characters in your favorite story?**

2. Stage directions tell actors what to do. **Why are stage directions important?**

3. A storyboard is a set of pictures that show the parts of a story in order. **Draw a storyboard that shows what you have done today.**

This is what author Clyde Robert Bulla thinks about words and writing: "Words are wonderful. By writing them and putting them together, I could make them say whatever I wanted to say. It was a kind of magic."

In this section, you will put words together in special ways in your own stories, plays, and poems. So, get ready . . . get set . . . imagine!

 Literature Connections: You can find a creative, add-on story in *Click, Clack, Moo: Cows That Type* by Doreen Cronin.

Writing
Add-On Stories

You can use your imagination by writing add-on stories. In Angela's add-on story, the main character has a problem. One by one, new characters are added to the story. In the end, something surprising happens, and the problem is solved.

Parts of a Story

Every story has four special parts: characters, setting, problem, and plot.

Characters	The characters are the people or animals in your story.
Setting	The setting tells the time and place of your story.
Problem	The problem is the trouble the characters face in the story.
Plot	The plot is the action in the story.

Angela's Add-On Story

Go Away, Clouds

Sun had a problem. She was shining, but no one could see her. Clouds were in the way.

Wind tried to help. He huffed and puffed. The clouds wouldn't move.

Then Moon came along. He said, "Go to sleep, Sun. When you wake, the clouds will be gone." Moon glowed all night. The clouds wouldn't move.

Finally, Wolf came along and howled at Moon. "Owoooo!" Suddenly, the clouds got scared and flew away.

In the morning, the clouds were gone. Sun felt happy because everyone could see her now.

After You Read

1. **Ideas** What are the four parts of the story? Who are the add-on characters?

Prewriting ▶ Selecting Your Topic

To get started, you need to think of a main character, a problem, and a setting for your add-on story. All stories *start* with these three parts.

Here's what Hunter did to start his add-on story.

Talk Hunter and a classmate talked about story ideas. They thought of characters and problems they could have.

Build Then Hunter built a questions chart, naming the main parts for his story. The chart answered the who, what, and where of his story.

Will your main character be a person, an animal, or an object like the sun?

Hunter's Story Questions Chart

Who is the main character?	rabbit
What problem happens?	stuck in a hole
When does the story happen?	morning
Where does the story happen?	outside

Prewrite ▶ **Select your topic.**

1. Talk about story ideas.
2. Build a story questions chart that answers the who, what, and where of your story.

Prewriting ▶ Gathering Details

Once you complete your questions chart, you can plan the plot or action for your story. You build the plot by adding characters who each try to help the main character.

This is what Hunter did to plan the plot for his add-on story.

Think   First, Hunter thought about characters who could help Rabbit.

Choose   From his thinking, he chose three characters to help rabbit.

Make   Next, Hunter made a story grid. He listed his characters and what they did.

I began with Rabbit. Then I added Ostrich, Little Kangaroo, and Python to my story.

Hunter's Story Grid

Character	Action
Ostrich	used her long neck to try to reach Rabbit
Little Kangaroo	jumped into the hole to try to save Rabbit
Python	tied himself to a tree and lowered himself into the hole

Prewrite ▶ **Gather details.**

1. Think about other characters and their actions.
2. Complete a story grid.

Writing ▶ Beginning Your Story

In the beginning paragraph, you should set up your story. Name the main character, the problem, and the setting.

Here's what Hunter did to write the beginning for his story.

▶ Beginning

Middle

Ending

Review First, Hunter reviewed his story questions chart. This chart names the main character, the problem, and the setting.

Name Hunter then wrote his first sentence. He decided to name the setting and main character in this sentence.

> One morning, Rabbit woke up and began digging.

Add He added more sentences that explained the problem.

Remember that the beginning paragraph sets up your story. It should sound interesting or exciting so that readers want to read on.

Hunter's Beginning

One morning, Rabbit woke up and began digging. He loved to dig, so he dug and dug a deep hole. When he was done, Rabbit had a problem. He couldn't get out!

Write ▶ **Begin your story.**

1. Review your story questions chart.
2. Write your first sentence naming the main character and setting.
3. Add more sentences that explain the main character's problem.

Writing ▸ Developing the Middle

In the middle part, you develop the plot or action of your add-on story. To do this, show how each new character tries to help the main character.

This is what Hunter did to develop the middle part of his story.

	Beginning
▸	**Middle**
	Ending

Review First, Hunter reviewed his story grid.

Show Then he showed how each new character tried to help Rabbit.

I used specific action verbs like *stretched* and *hissed* and dialogue to make this part fun to read.

Write ▸ **Develop the middle.**

1. Review your story grid.
2. Show how each new character tries to help.

Hunter wrote about each new character in a different paragraph. This makes his story easy to follow.

Hunter's Middle Part

"Help me!" Rabbit cried.

Ostrich heard him and looked into the hole. She stretched her long neck and tried to reach Rabbit. Her neck was not long enough.

Little Kangaroo came along. She hopped into the hole. "Jump into my pocket, and we will hop out," she said. Rabbit was too heavy. Little Kangaroo jumped out alone.

"Sssss," someone hissed. It was Python. He said, "I know what to do." He tied himself to a tree to make a long rope. Then Rabbit climbed up Python and out of the hole.

Writing ▶ Ending Your Story

In the ending part, you should tell how your main character feels when the problem is finally solved.

Here's how Hunter completed his add-on story.

Beginning

Middle

▶ **Ending**

Think   First, Hunter thought how his main character would feel.

Write   Then he wrote his ending.
1. The first sentence tells how Rabbit felt.
2. The second sentence tells how the problem changed him.

I decided that my main character would feel excited.

Hunter's ending paragraph comes after the problem is solved. It tells what the main character learned.

Hunter's Ending

> Rabbit was excited to be out of the hole. He said, "I'll never dig that deep again."

You could turn your add-on story into a book with pictures.

Write ▶ End your story.

1. Think how the main character would feel after the problem is solved.
2. Write at least two sentences. In the first one, tell how your main character feels. In the next sentence, tell how he or she has changed.

Revising ▶ Improving Your Writing

When revising, check that your add-on story is clear and complete.

Here's how Hunter revised his story.

Check   Hunter checked his first draft using the checklist below as a guide.

Did you review?

✔ 1. Does the beginning name the main character with a problem?

✔ 2. Does the middle add on characters and their actions?

✔ 3. Does the last action solve the problem?

✔ 4. Does the ending tell how the main character felt?

Make   He then made any needed changes.

Revise ▶ Improve your writing.

1. Check your story using the checklist above.
2. Make any needed changes.

Editing ▸ **Checking for Conventions**

When editing your paragraph, you check your writing for capitalization, punctuation, and spelling.

Here's how Hunter edited his story.

Check Hunter edited his story using the checklist below as a guide.

Did you check?

✓ 1. Did you capitalize names and the first word in each sentence?

✓ 2. Did you use a punctuation mark after each sentence?

✓ 3. Did you check for spelling?

Correct Then he corrected any errors.

Edit ▸ **Make the needed corrections.**

1. Check your story for conventions using the checklist above as a guide.
2. Correct any errors.

Publishing ▶ Sharing Your Story

Write a neat final copy of your story to share.

Rabbit's Big Mistake

One morning, Rabbit woke up and began digging. He loved to dig, so he dug and dug a deep hole. When he was done, Rabbit had a problem. He couldn't get out!

"Help me!" Rabbit cried.

Ostrich heard him and looked into the hole. She stretched her long neck and tried to reach Rabbit. Her neck was not long enough.

Little Kangaroo came along. She hopped into the hole. "Jump into my pocket, and we will hop out," she said. Rabbit was too heavy. Little Kangaroo jumped out alone.

"Sssssss," someone hissed. It was Python. He said, "I know what to do." He tied himself to a tree to make a long rope. Then Rabbit climbed up Python and out of the hole.

Rabbit was excited to be out of the hole. He said, "I'll never dig that deep again."

Publish ▶ **Share your story.**

Adding Up the Elements of Stories

The words and ideas below describe the main parts of stories.

Action The action is what happens in a story.

Character A character is a person or an animal in a story.

Dialogue Dialogue is what characters say to each other.

Fiction Fiction is a made-up story.

Moral A moral is the lesson that a story teaches.

Plot The plot is what happens.

Problem The problem is the trouble in a story.

Setting The setting is the time and place of a story.

Theme The theme is the main idea or message in a story.

Creating a Play

Plays are fun to write because the writer decides what the characters say and do. Jade turned the nursery rhyme below into a play.

In this chapter, you, too, will learn how to write a play based on a nursery rhyme.

Polly Put the Kettle On

Polly put the kettle on.
Polly put the kettle on.
Polly put the kettle on.
We'll all have tea.
Suki take it off again.
Suki take it off again.
Suki take it off again.
They've all gone away.

Dialogue is what the characters say.
Stage Directions tell what the characters do and feel.

Jade's Play

Where Did Everybody Go?

Characters: Polly and Suki
Setting: It is afternoon. Polly
and Suki are in the house.

Dialogue

Suki: Look! Visitors are coming. Polly, put the kettle on. Polly, put the kettle on. Polly, put the kettle on. We'll all have tea.

Polly: (making tea) How many are there? How much tea should I make? (Polly runs to the window to see.)

Stage Directions

Polly: Suki, take it off again. Suki, take it off again. Suki, take it off again. They've all gone away!

Suki: (looking out window) What? Where did everybody go?

Prewriting ▶ Selecting a Topic

To get started, select a nursery rhyme that you would like to turn into a play.

This is what Marta did to select a topic.

Think Marta thought about the nursery rhymes that her class read.

List She listed her favorite ones.

List of Topics

Baa Baa Black Sheep

Simple Simon

Five Little Ducks

Rose and the Lily

Choose a nursery rhyme that has at least two characters in it.

Circle Then Marta circled the rhyme she wanted to turn into a play.

 Prewrite ▶ **Select a topic.**

1. List your favorite nursery rhymes.
2. Circle the one you will turn into a play.

Gathering Details

To plan your play, think about the characters you will include. Also think about the setting of your play.

Here's what Marta did to gather her first details for her play.

Make First, Marta made a T-chart. She labeled one side *characters* and the other side *settings*.

Name Next, she listed the characters and setting for her play.

Details T-Chart

Characters	Setting
1. Simple Simon	Time: Summer
2. pieman	Place: On the way to the fair

Prewrite ▶ **Gather details.**

1. Make a T-chart.
2. Name the characters and setting for your play.

Prewriting ▶ Putting Events in Order

The next step is to think of the important events that happen in the nursery rhyme. Knowing these events will help you write your play.

Storyboard

Here's what Marta did to plan the action for her play.

Read Marta read the nursery rhyme so that she knew what happened.

Draw Then Marta drew pictures of the important events in the nursery rhyme. She put the events in time order in a storyboard.

first

Making a storyboard helped me plan the different actions and dialogue in my play.

Your storyboard should have at least four boxes. Otherwise, you may not have enough details to write a play.

Marta ordered her storyboard with the time-order words **first, next, then,** and **last**.

next

then

last

? ? ?

Can I have a taste?

Do you have a penny?

Does anyone have a penny?

Prewrite ▶ **Plan a storyboard.**

1. Read the nursery rhyme.
2. Draw a storyboard of the events in the nursery rhyme.

Writing ▶ Beginning Your Play

In the beginning part, name the characters and the setting of your play. Also tell what is happening as the play starts.

This is what Marta did to write the beginning part of her play.

Beginning

Middle

Ending

Review First, Marta reviewed her T-chart from page 229.

Characters	Setting
1. Simple Simon	Time: Summer
2. pieman	Place: On the way to the fair

Write Next, she wrote sentences that tell who the characters are and what is happening.

Plays are fun to write and even more fun to perform. (See page 241.)

The beginning part of Marta's play helps the reader picture who is in the play, where they are, and what they are doing.

Marta's Beginning

Characters: Simple Simon and a pieman

Setting: It is summer. The place is on the way to the fair. Along the way, Simple Simon meets a pieman.

Write ▶ **Begin your play.**

1. Review your T-chart from page 229.
2. Write a sentence that tells who the characters are and what is happening to start your play.

Writing ▶ Developing the Middle

In the middle part, you tell your story by having the characters talk to each other. You also include stage directions when they are needed.

This is what Marta did to develop the middle part of her play.

Beginning

▶ **Middle**

Ending

Review Marta reviewed her story-board. (See pages 230–231.)

first

next

then

last

Can I have a taste?

Do you have a penny?

Does anyone have a penny?

Write Then she wrote the middle part of her play.

The characters tell the story, so their words are the most important part of my play.

In Marta's play, the stage directions, in parentheses, tell what the characters do or feel.

Marta's Main Part

Simple Simon: (shakes hands with the pieman)
Your pies look yummy.

Pieman: Would you like to buy one?

Simple Simon: No. I would like to taste
one piece.

Pieman: It will cost a penny for a taste.

Simple Simon: (looks through pockets and
shoes) I don't have a penny.

Pieman: Then no pie for you.

Simple Simon: Not even a taste?

Pieman: No penny. No taste. No pie!

Write ▶ **Develop the middle.**

1. Review your storyboard.
2. Write the middle part of your play.

Writing ▶ Ending Your Play

In the ending of your play, have the main character say one last important thing.

This is what Marta did to write the ending for her play.

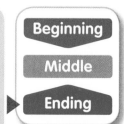

Beginning

Middle

Ending

Read Marta read the middle part of her play to help her decide what the main character should say and do in the ending.

Write Then she wrote the main character's last line and added stage directions.

Add Next, Marta added a title. She tried two ways to write it.

1. **Name the characters.**

Simon and the Pieman

2. **Use a topic detail.**

Just One Tiny Taste

Marta's ending fits in with the nursery rhyme and the rest of her play.

Marta's Ending

Simple Simon: (walking off stage, calls
to other people going
to the fair) Does anyone
have a penny so I can
try some pie?

In my ending, I first gave stage directions. Then I had Simple Simon ask a final question.

Write ▶ **End your play.**

1. Read the middle part of your play.
2. Write the main character's last line. Also add stage directions if needed.

Revising ▶ Improving Your Play

Revise your play to be sure it is clear and easy to follow.

Here's what Marta did to revise her play.

Review Marta reviewed her first draft using the questions below as a guide.

1. Does your beginning tell what is happening as the play starts?
2. In the middle, did you write each character's name before her or his words?
3. Did you have the main character say something important in the ending?

Make She then made the needed changes so her play was clear.

Revise ▶ **Improve your play.**

1. Check your play using the questions above as a guide.
2. Make any needed changes.

Editing ▶ **Checking for Conventions**

Edit your play to be sure it is free of errors.

This is what Marta did to edit her play.

Check Marta checked her play for conventions using the checklist below as a guide.

Correct She then corrected any convention errors.

Did you check?

✔ 1. Did you capitalize the names and the first words of sentences?

✔ 2. Did you end sentences with correct punctuation?

✔ 3. Did you check your spelling?

Edit ▶ **Check for conventions.**

1. Check your play for conventions using the checklist above as a guide.
2. Correct any errors.

Publishing ▶ Sharing Your Play

Just One Tiny Taste

Characters: Simple Simon and a pieman
Setting: It is summer. The place is on the way to the fair. Along the way to the fair, Simple Simon meets a pieman.

Simple Simon: (shakes hands with the pieman) Your pies look yummy.

Pieman: Would you like to buy one?

Simple Simon: No. I would like to taste one piece.

Pieman: It will cost a penny for a taste.

Simple Simon: (looks through pockets and shoes) I don't have a penny.

Pieman: Then no pie for you.

Simple Simon: Not even a taste?

Pieman: No penny. No taste. No pie!

Simple Simon: (walking off stage, calls to other people going to the fair) Does anyone have a penny so I can try some pie?

Publish ▶ **Share your play.**

Performing a Play

You can perform your play by reading it to your classmates. You can also form a team and perform your play as a group. Follow the steps below.

Select   Select a classmate for each character and for a narrator. (See below.)

Give   Give each team member a copy of the play, and decide who gets each part.

Practice   Practice reading the play and following the stage directions.

Perform   Perform the play by reading it to your audience. (Speak the play if you memorized it.) Follow the stage directions as you go.

The narrator shares the opening part to set the scene for the play.

Narrator: "Just One Tiny Taste" takes place in the summer. Along the way to the fair, Simple Simon meets a pieman.

Writing Poems

Poems come in all shapes and sizes. Some poems rhyme. Some poems follow a certain shape. Other poems even follow the alphabet!

Alec has fun writing poems. He especially likes writing rhyming poems and name poems. You can write these poems, too. This chapter will show you how.

Each pair of rhyming lines should include close to the same number of words.

Alec's Rhyming Poem

Riding

My bike is more fun than TV or a slide.

The tires spin fast wherever I ride.

Kids jump aside when I rush by.

Riding my bike makes me one happy guy.

After You Read

1. **Ideas** What is the main idea of this poem?
2. **Organization** Which lines of the poem rhyme?
3. **Word Choice** Which detail do you like best?

Prewriting ▶ Choosing a Topic

Writing a rhyming poem can be fun. To get started, think of an activity that you would like to write about.

Here's what Shayna did to select a topic for her poem.

Draw Shayna drew pictures of her favorite activities.

State Then she stated the topic for her poem in a sentence.

Pictures of Activities

I will write my poem about dancing.

Prewrite ▶ **Choose a topic.**

1. Draw pictures of activities you enjoy.
2. State the topic for your poem in a sentence.

Gathering Details

Gather many details about your activity. This will help you decide what to say in your poem.

This is what Shayna did to gather details.

Think First, Shayna thought about the sights and sounds related to the activity.

Make Then she wrote sentences about dancing for different sensory words.

Sensory Sentences

Dancing

I see the world spin when I twirl.

I hear music with a Latin beat.

I smell fresh air when I dance outside.

I feel the wind when I dance.

 **Prewrite** ▶ **Gather details.**

1. Think about your activity.
2. Write sentences about the activity for different sensory words.

Prewriting ▶ Listing Rhyming Words

Before you write your first draft, you should think of rhyming words that you can use in your poem.

This is what Shayna did to gather rhyming words for her poem.

Choose Shayna chose special words from her sensory chart. She wrote them across the top of her paper.

List Then she listed words that rhyme with each special word.

List of Rhyming Words

dance	twirl	beat	spin
prance	girl	neat	win
chance	whirl	treat	chin
France	swirl	feet	grin

Prewrite ▶ **List rhyming words.**

1. Choose special words from your sensory chart and write them across the top of your paper.
2. List words that rhyme with each special word.

Writing ▶ Writing Your First Draft

Write a poem about the activity. Use rhyming words at the end of each pair of lines.

Here's how Shayna wrote her rhyming poem.

Choose Shayna chose to write a rhyming poem in four lines.

Use She used rhyming words at the end of the first two lines and at the end of the last two lines. She looked at her rhyming words list for ideas.

Sample Rhyming Lines

I love to dance to a drumming beat.
I clap my hands and stomp my feet.

Write ▶ **Write your first draft.**

1. Decide how many lines to write.
2. Use rhyming words at the end of each pair of lines. Look at your rhyming list for ideas.

Revising ▶ Improving Your Poem

Make sure that your poem is fun to read. Each pair of lines should sound good together.

This is what Shayna did to revise her rhyming poem.

Use   Shayna used the following checklist to help her review her poem.

Did you review?

✓ 1. Did you write about one activity?

✓ 2. Did you make each pair of lines rhyme?

✓ 3. Did you include close to the same number of words for each set of rhyming lines?

Make   Then she made any needed changes.

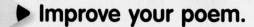

Revise ▶ **Improve your poem.**

1. Use the checklist above to review your poem.
2. Make any needed changes.

Editing ▸ Checking for Conventions

Correct copy is easier and more fun to read. Checking your poem for conventions is important.

This is how Shayna edited her poem.

Check Shayna checked her poem for conventions. She used the checklist below as a guide.

Did you check?

✓ 1. Did you capitalize names and the first words of sentences?

✓ 2. Did you end sentences with correct punctuation?

✓ 3. Did you check for spelling?

Correct She then corrected any convention errors.

Edit ▸ **Check for conventions.**

1. Check your poem for conventions using the questions above as a guide.
2. Correct any errors.

Publishing ▶ Sharing Your Poem

Shayna's Poem

Shayna Dancing

I love dancing to a Latin beat.
I clap my hands and stomp my feet.
I feel the wind as I spin and twirl.
Look! I'm a happy dancing girl!

Publish ▶ **Make a neat final copy.**

1. Add a title and make a neat copy of your poem.
2. Read your poem to family and friends.

Creating a Name Poem

A name poem uses the letters in a name to make a list poem.

This is how you start your name poem.

Write Write your name across the top of a piece of paper.

List List three or more describing words for each letter.

Describing Words

S	E	A	N
smart	excited	amusing	nice
scientist	empties the trash	actor	nickname is Champ
speaks Spanish	explores the beach	age 8 an amigo	never naughty

Completing Your Name Poem

To write your name poem, use describing words from your list. Try to use close to the same number of words in each line.

This is how you write, revise, and publish your poem.

Choose   Choose describing words from your chart. Use one or more words in each line.

Check   Check your poem for capitalization and spelling.

Make   Make a neat final copy to share.

Sean's Name Poem

Speaks Spanish
Explores the beach
Amigo to everyone
Nickname is Champ

Other Kinds of Poems

Try writing these other kinds of poems, too.

ABC Poem

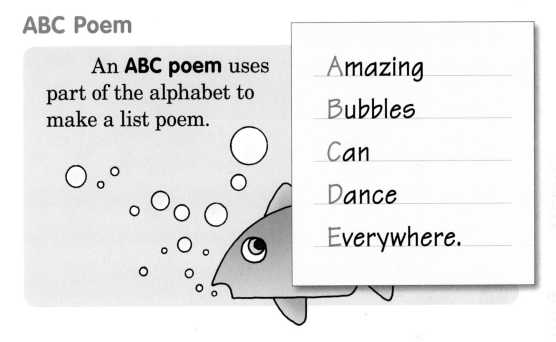

An **ABC poem** uses part of the alphabet to make a list poem.

Amazing
Bubbles
Can
Dance
Everywhere.

Tongue Twister

A **tongue twister** is a short, silly story poem. Most of the words begin with the same sound. This is called **alliteration**.

Wet weather brings
wonderful worms who
wiggle wildly. Wow!

Shape Poem

A **shape poem** uses the words of the poem to make the shape of the poem's main idea.

There's a fish! Jumping, splashing, swimming, swish, swish, swish, swish. Look down in the river!

Terse Verse

Terse verse is short and funny. It has two rhyming words that have the same number of syllables. The title is the subject.

Huge Hog

Big
Pig

Lemonade

Pink
Drink

Joke Book

Smile
File

Diamond Poem

This **diamond poem** follows a syllable pattern. (Lines two and six name the subject.)

one
two
three
four
three
two
one

bats
baseball
pitch hit run
bases loaded
first home run
baseball
cheers

5 W's Poem

A **5 W's poem** is five lines long. Each line answers one of the 5 W's (*Who? What? When? Where?* and *Why?*).

My dog
curls up
on my bed
every night
because I let him.

Who?
What?
Where?
When?
Why?

Report Writing

Writing Focus

- Finding Information
- Writing a Report
- Multimedia Presentation

Academic Vocabulary

Work with a partner. Read the meanings and share answers to the questions.

1. A **reference** is a book or other source that is used to find information.
   Why is a dictionary a good reference?

2. When you **improve** something, you make it better.
   What could you improve about your desk?

3. A **presentation** is a showing that often uses slides or video.
   What presentations have you seen at your school?

What do you do when you have a question? Of course, you can ask your teachers and parents. You can also go to the library to find an answer. In this section, you will learn how to find information, write a report, and create a multimedia presentation.

 Literature Connections: You can find an example of report writing in *Dogs* by Jennifer Blizin Gillis.

Finding Information

Ezra and his class were getting ready to write reports. Each student had to choose a bird to write about. Their teacher took the students to the library to learn how to find information for their reports.

The class learned a lot about using the library. You will, too, on the pages that follow.

The Librarian

The librarian knows all about finding information. Be sure to ask the librarian for help whenever you have a question about the library.

What does a librarian do?

A librarian

- chooses and organizes the library's books.
- helps you find information.
- knows where everything is in the library.
- helps you with computer searches.
- shows you books and stories you might like.

Sections of a Library

Libraries may look different from one another, but they all contain the same types of books and material. On this page and the next, you will find an example map of a library.

Library Map

Fiction: This is where you'll find stories and chapter books.

Fiction

Nonfiction: This section has books about real people, places, and things.

Nonfiction

Reference: This is where the atlases, encyclopedias, and dictionaries are kept.

Reference

Checkout Desk

Beginner Books: This is where the picture books are.

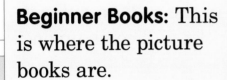

Beginner Books

Computer or Card Catalog

Periodicals

Media Section

Computer or Card Catalog: This section tells you the titles of every book in the library!

Periodicals: This is where you will find magazines and newspapers.

Media Section: This area has CD's, DVD's, and computers.

The Computer Catalog

A computer catalog gives you three ways to look up a book in a library.

1. If you know the **title** of a book, enter it.
2. If you know the name of the **author**, enter it. A list of the author's books will come up on the computer screen.
3. To find a book on a certain **subject**, enter the subject or a keyword.

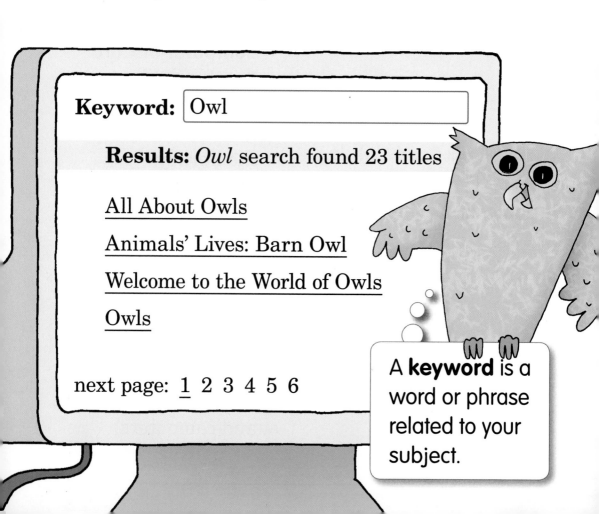

Keyword: Owl

Results: *Owl* search found 23 titles

All About Owls

Animals' Lives: Barn Owl

Welcome to the World of Owls

Owls

next page: <u>1</u> 2 3 4 5 6

A **keyword** is a word or phrase related to your subject.

The Card Catalog

Some libraries keep the information about their books on cards contained in a big file cabinet. Every book has a **title**, an **author**, and a **subject** card. The cards are filed in ABC order.

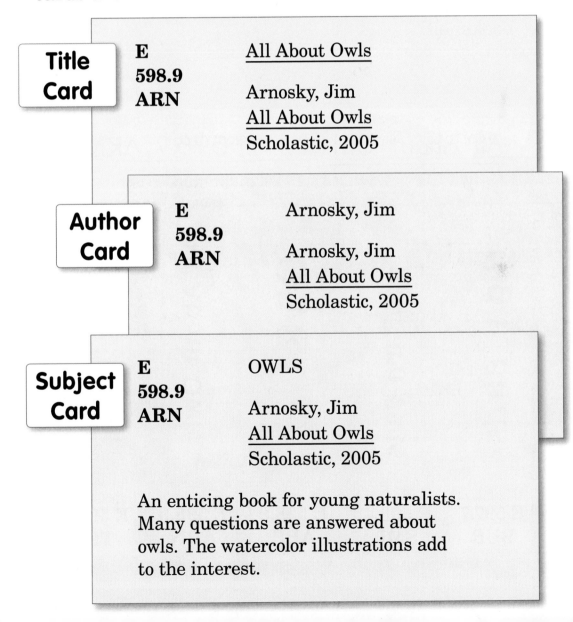

Title Card

E
598.9
ARN

All About Owls

Arnosky, Jim
All About Owls
Scholastic, 2005

Author Card

E
598.9
ARN

Arnosky, Jim

Arnosky, Jim
All About Owls
Scholastic, 2005

Subject Card

E
598.9
ARN

OWLS

Arnosky, Jim
All About Owls
Scholastic, 2005

An enticing book for young naturalists. Many questions are answered about owls. The watercolor illustrations add to the interest.

Call Numbers

To find a nonfiction book, carefully write down the **call number** from the catalog. Ask the librarian to help you find the book. The picture below shows how to find *All About Owls* on the bookshelf.

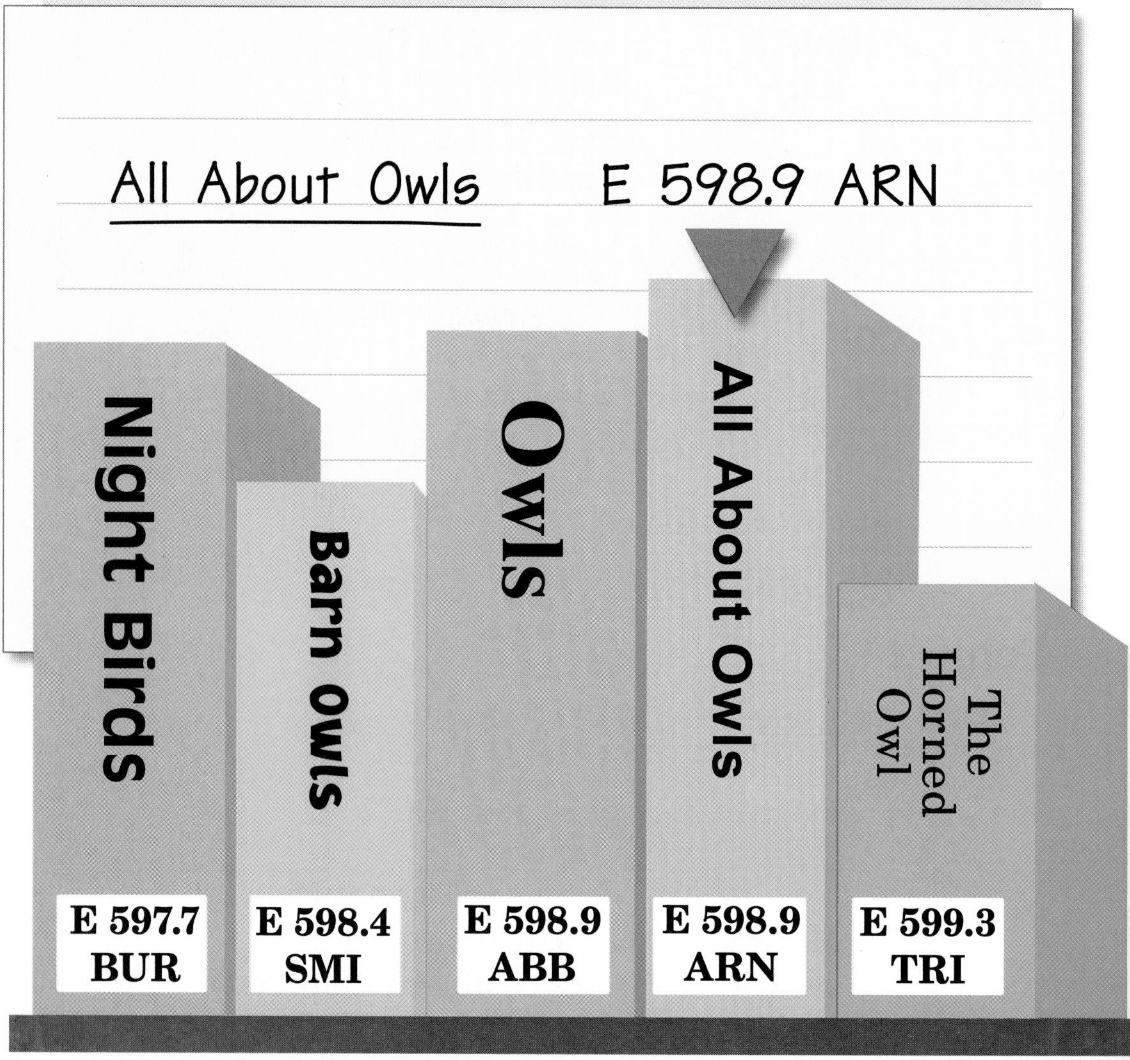

All About Owls   E 598.9 ARN

Night Birds	Barn Owls	Owls	All About Owls	The Horned Owl
E 597.7 BUR	E 598.4 SMI	E 598.9 ABB	E 598.9 ARN	E 599.3 TRI

Parts of a Book

Every book is made up of different parts. Some of these parts give publishing information; other parts help you find chapters or topics in the book.

Front of the Book

- The **title page** lists the book's title and author. It may also list the illustrator.

- The **table of contents** lists the chapters and their page numbers.

Back of the Book

- A **glossary** lists words from the book and their meanings.

- The **index** lists topics from the book in ABC order and gives you their page numbers.

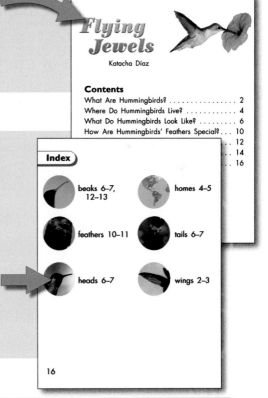

Flying Jewels

Katacha Díaz

Contents

Index

beaks 6–7, 12–13

homes 4–5

feathers 10–11

tails 6–7

heads 6–7

wings 2–3

16

practice

Use the index in this book to locate information about editing and proofreading marks.

Encyclopedia

Encyclopedias are books that contain articles on many topics. The topics are arranged in ABC order. To find information about owls, look in the O book.

Electronic Encyclopedia

Encyclopedias are also found on CD's or on the Internet. Ask your teacher or the librarian to help you use this type of encyclopedia.

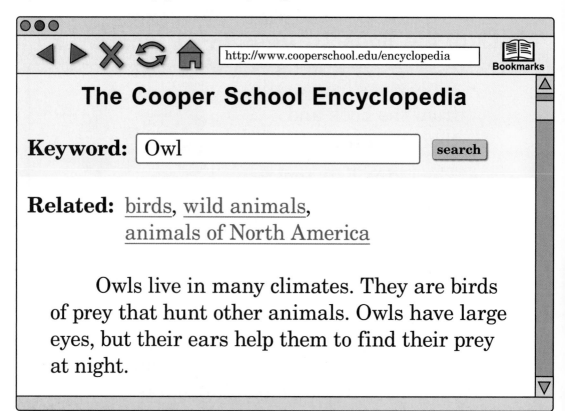

http://www.cooperschool.edu/encyclopedia

Bookmarks

The Cooper School Encyclopedia

Keyword: Owl   [search]

Related: birds, wild animals, animals of North America

Owls live in many climates. They are birds of prey that hunt other animals. Owls have large eyes, but their ears help them to find their prey at night.

Thesaurus

If you want to find another word for *turn*, you can look in a thesaurus. Different words that mean the same thing are called **synonyms**. A thesaurus lists words in ABC order.

Owls turn their heads to search for food.

Thesaurus entry

turn   verb 1. The hands on the clock turn. *circle, spin, swivel*

Choosing a Synonym

You can use the synonym *swivel* instead of the word *turn*. *Swivel* is more specific and descriptive.

Owls swivel their heads to search for food.

Using a thesaurus can help you with  .

Dictionary

Dictionaries are found in the reference section. A dictionary tells you many things about words.

Guide Words — These words are found at the top of each page. They show the first and last entry words.

Entry Word — These are the words listed in ABC order on each page.

Spelling — Each entry word is spelled correctly.

Meaning — The meaning or meanings of each entry word are given.

Example Sentence — Each entry word is used in a sentence.

Some dictionaries show the pronunciation of a word.

ca • nar • y (kə nâŕ ē)

Sample Dictionary Page

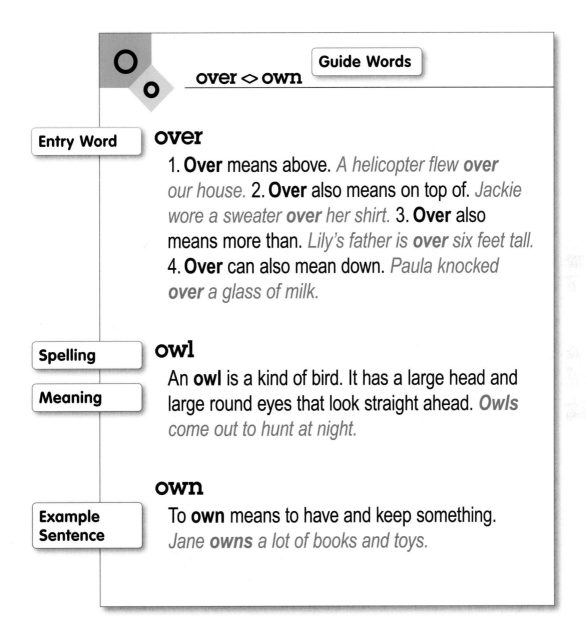

Guide Words

over ◇ own

Entry Word

over

1. **Over** means above. *A helicopter flew over our house.* 2. **Over** also means on top of. *Jackie wore a sweater over her shirt.* 3. **Over** also means more than. *Lily's father is over six feet tall.* 4. **Over** can also mean down. *Paula knocked over a glass of milk.*

Spelling

Meaning

owl

An **owl** is a kind of bird. It has a large head and large round eyes that look straight ahead. *Owls come out to hunt at night.*

Example Sentence

own

To **own** means to have and keep something. *Jane owns a lot of books and toys.*

World Wide Web

Another source of information is the World Wide Web. For example, the Web sites for zoos and rescue centers would probably have interesting details about owls.

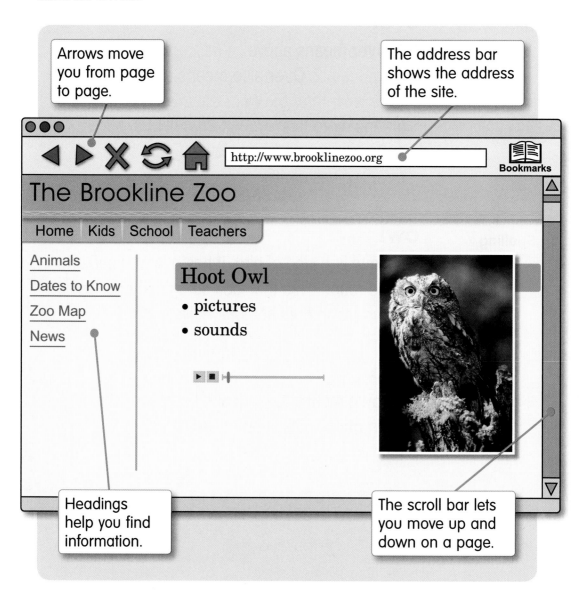

Arrows move you from page to page.

The address bar shows the address of the site.

http://www.brooklinezoo.org

Bookmarks

The Brookline Zoo

Home   Kids   School   Teachers

Animals
Dates to Know
Zoo Map
News

Hoot Owl
• pictures
• sounds

Headings help you find information.

The scroll bar lets you move up and down on a page.

Periodicals

Magazines and newspapers are good sources of up-to-date information. New editions come out every month, every week, or every day. See the sample magazine pages below.

Cover

Date — May 2009

Owl World

The Who's Whoooo in the Bird Kingdom

Table of Contents

Table of Contents

The Bird's Word 5
Better Barns for Owls 7
From Nest to Egg 18
Burrowing Owls of the Dakotas 25

Page number

Article

7

Better Barns for Owls
by Bo Birdwatcher

Title

Author

Some barns make better homes than others. To attract owls to your barn, there are some simple tips you can follow.

Writing a Report

In a report, you can share what you learn about an interesting topic. Tori wrote a report about hummingbirds. It is one of her best pieces of writing. You can write a report, too. This chapter will show you how.

Tori's Report

Humming Wonders

Beginning

A hummingbird is an amazing bird. When it flies, its wings go so fast that they hum. That is how the bird got its name. A hummingbird can fly up, down, forward, and even backward.

Middle

The hummingbird is tiny. It is about 3 1/2 inches long. Its feathers are mostly brown and gray, but some are a shiny green, purple, red, or orange.

Tori's Report (continued)

Middle

When a hummingbird eats, it flies like a helicopter. It pokes its long beak into flowers and drinks nectar. A hummingbird likes orange and red flowers. It also eats tree sap and insects. It lives close to the water in forests and gardens.

Middle

The mother bird builds a small nest out of tiny sticks and spiderwebs. She fills the nest with dandelion fluff and cattail fuzz. Then she lays two white eggs. The eggs are the size of peas.

Middle   When the chicks hatch, they have no feathers. They are very tiny. The mother gathers insects, sap, and nectar to feed her babies. They grow fast. In two or three weeks, they can fly!

Ending   A hummingbird seems very smart. The spiderwebs let the nest stretch as the babies grow! I like the hummingbird because it is shiny, beautiful, and amazing.

Prewriting ▶ Choosing Your Topic

Choosing a topic is the first thing you do in report writing.

Tori's class brainstormed about different birds. Their teacher wrote the bird's names on the board. Tori decided to write about hummingbirds. She had watched them in her grandmother's yard.

Topic Ideas

owl	bobwhite	
eagle	hummingbird	
bluebird	pelican	
flamingo	jay	duck
parrot	kiwi	heron
penguin	tern	pigeon

I am really interested in hummingbirds.

Prewrite ▶ **Choose your topic.**

1. Pick a bird to write about. (Or pick a different topic if your teacher directs you to do so.)
2. Decide on a topic that truly interests you.

Finding Sources

Finding sources about your topic is the next step.

Tori asked her teacher and the librarian for help finding her sources of information. Then Tori listed the sources she found in the following way.

Source List

Books	Hummingbirds by Diane Swanson
	Birds by Claude Delafosse
Magazine	Birdwatcher's Digest
Internet	www.hummingbirds.net

 Prewrite ▶ Find sources.

1. Ask your teacher or librarian for help.
2. Find books, magazines, and Web sites about your bird.
3. Make a list of sources, like the list above.

Prewriting ▶ Gathering Details

Making a gathering grid can help you to gather details.

To make a grid, Tori folded a large sheet of paper into eight squares and wrote a heading in each. Then she listed facts under each heading.

Gathering Grid

1. What the Bird Looks Like	2. What It Eats
• long pointy beak • shiny green, purple, red, orange, brown, and gray feathers • wings go fast • 3 1/2 inches long	• nectar from red and orange flowers • tree sap and insects • fly and eat at the same time
5. The Nest	6. The Eggs
• built by mother bird • filled with cattail fuzz and dandelion fluff • tiny sticks and spiderwebs	• white • lays two eggs • size of a pea

3. Where It Lives

- in mountains, forests, gardens
- near water

4. Some Amazing Facts

- the nest can stretch
- fly up, down, backward, and forward very fast
- wings hum when they fly

7. The Babies

- born with no feathers
- fly in 2 or 3 weeks

8. I like this bird because

- beautiful, tiny birds
- fun to watch

Prewrite ▶ **Gather details.**

1. Make your own gathering grid.
2. List facts under each heading.

Interviewing Someone

Other people may know about your topic. Tori decided to interview her grandmother, who loves to watch hummingbirds.

Interview Tips

Before the Interview

Think of a person who knows about your topic.

With a parent's help, **set up a time** to interview this person.

Write questions you would like to ask. Leave space after each to write the answers.

During the Interview

Ask questions and listen carefully.

Write the answers on your paper.

After the Interview

Thank the person for talking with you.

Write facts from your notes onto your grid. (See pages 278–279.)

Tori's Interview

1. What do hummingbirds eat?
   —sap and insects
   —drink nectar with a long tongue

2. Where have you seen hummingbirds?
   —at the feeder on the porch
   —by the lake on orange lilies

3. Why do you like hummingbirds?
   —colored like shiny, bright jewels

4. What is your favorite thing about the hummingbird?
   —fun to watch

 **Prewrite**   ▶ **Interview someone.**

1. Decide on someone to interview about your topic.
2. Plan and carry out the interview.

Writing ▶ Beginning Your Report

The beginning part of a report should get the reader's interest and introduce your topic.

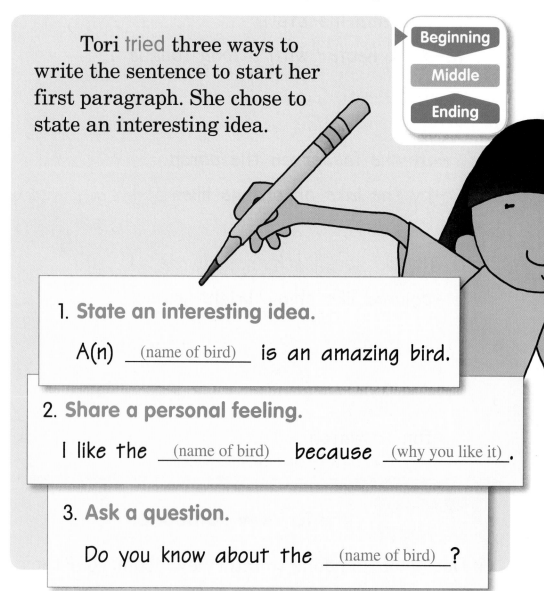

Tori tried three ways to write the sentence to start her first paragraph. She chose to state an interesting idea.

Beginning
Middle
Ending

1. **State an interesting idea.**

   A(n) _(name of bird)_ is an amazing bird.

2. **Share a personal feeling.**

   I like the _(name of bird)_ because _(why you like it)_ .

3. **Ask a question.**

   Do you know about the _(name of bird)_ ?

Tori started her first paragraph with an interesting idea. Then she used two amazing facts from her grid to support the first sentence. Her goal was to make her topic sound really interesting.

> The beginning paragraph introduces the topic and shares interesting facts.

Tori's Beginning Paragraph

A hummingbird is an amazing bird. Its wings go so fast that they hum. That is how it got its name. A hummingbird can fly up, down, forward, and even backward.

Write ▶ **Write your beginning.**

1. Use your best first sentence to start your beginning paragraph.
2. Add two or three interesting facts from your grid. These sentences should support the beginning sentence.

Writing ▶ Creating the Middle Part

Your middle paragraphs should explain and describe your topic.

Tori first made groups of main ideas from her grid and put them in order. Then she wrote her middle paragraphs. She wrote about a different main idea in each paragraph. She included ideas from her grid in each paragraph.

Beginning

▶ Middle

Ending

Tori's Main Ideas

1. Describe the bird's body.
2. Tell about food and where it lives.
3. Tell about its nest and eggs.
4. Tell about the babies.

Tori used a lot of details from her grid in this paragraph.

Tori's First Middle Paragraph

The hummingbird is tiny. It is about 3 1/2 inches long. Its feathers are mostly brown and gray, but some are a shiny green, purple, red, or orange.

Write ▶ Create the middle part.

1. Make four main idea groups from your grid. (Or use Tori's main ideas.)

2. Write a paragraph for each main group. Use details from your grid.

Writing ▸ Ending Your Report

Your ending paragraph should bring your report to a close.

Tori reviewed her ideas from her grid for any amazing details she hadn't used. She started the final paragraph with one of these ideas. Then she finished her paragraph by telling why she likes hummingbirds.

Beginning

Middle

▸ Ending

Ending Ideas

4. Some Amazing Facts

- the nest can stretch
- fly up, down, backward, and forward very fast
- wings hum when they fly

8. I like this bird because

- beautiful, tiny birds
- fun to watch

Tori's Ending Paragraph

> A hummingbird seems very smart. The spiderwebs let the nest stretch as the babies grow! I like the hummingbird because it is shiny, beautiful, and amazing.

Write ▶ **End your report.**

1. List interesting ideas from your grid that you haven't used yet.
2. Start with an amazing idea from your list.
3. Finish your paragraph by telling why you like your topic.

Revising ▶ Improving Your Report

When you revise, you change any parts that seem unclear or incomplete.

To revise, Tori first read her report out loud. She used a checklist to help her check for ideas, organization, and sentence fluency. Then she made the needed changes.

Did you check?

✔ 1. Did you focus on one bird?

✔ 2. Did you include specific details about the topic?

Ideas

✔ 3. Did you write a beginning, a middle, and an ending?

✔ 4. Did you include one main idea in each paragraph?

Organization

✔ 5. Did you write complete sentences?

✔ 6. Did you use short and long sentences?

Sentence Fluency

Tori combined two sentences, fixed a fragment, and replaced a general word with specific details.

Tori's Revising

The Mother bird builds a small
nest, ~~The mother bird builds it~~ out
of tiny sticks and spiderwebs. She
fills the nest with dandylion fluff
and cattail fuzz. Then ∧she lays two white
eggs. The eggs are the size of peas.

When the chicks hatch, they
have no feathers. They are very tiny.
The mother gathers ∧insects sap and nectar ~~food~~ to feed
her babies. They grow fast. In two or
three weeks, they can fly!

Revise ▶ **Improve your report.**

Use the checklist on page 288 to review your report and make the needed changes.

Editing ▸ **Checking Your Conventions**

After revising, check your report for conventions. Correct any capitalization, punctuation, and spelling errors.

Tori edited her report for conventions using the checklist below as a guide. Next, she corrected any errors she found.

Conventions

Did you check?

✔ 1. Did you indent the beginning of each paragraph?

✔ 2. Did you capitalize the first word in each sentence?

✔ 3. Did you capitalize names?

✔ 4. Did you put an end punctuation mark after each sentence?

✔ 5. Did you use commas between words in a series?

✔ 6. Did you check your spelling?

Tori corrected a capitalization error and a spelling error, and added commas between words in a series.

Tori's Editing

m
The Mother bird builds a small nest out of tiny sticks and spiderwebs. She fills the nest with ~~dandylion~~ *dandelion* fluff and cattail fuzz. Then she lays two white eggs. The eggs are the size of peas.

When the chicks hatch, they have no feathers. They are very tiny. The mother gathers insects, sap, and nectar to feed her babies. They grow fast. In two or three weeks, they can fly!

Edit ▶ **Check for conventions.**

1. Edit your report for conventions.
2. Correct any errors you find.

Publishing ▶ Sharing Your Final Copy

You can neatly print your report, or you can make a final copy on a computer.

Tori used a computer to make a final copy of her report. She shared it with her class.

Tori's Final Report

Humming Wonders

A hummingbird is an amazing bird. When it flies, its wings go so fast that they hum. That is how the bird got its name. A hummingbird can fly up, down, forward, and even backward.

The hummingbird is tiny. It is about 3 1/2 inches long. Its feathers are mostly brown and gray, but some are a shiny green, purple, red, or orange.

When a hummingbird eats, it flies like a helicopter. It pokes its long beak into flowers and drinks nectar. A hummingbird likes orange and red flowers. It also eats tree sap and insects. It lives close to the

ests and gardens. her bird builds a ut of tiny sticks and . She fills the nest with uff and cattail fuzz. ys two white eggs. The e size of peas. e chicks hatch, they hers. They are very ther gathers insects, ctar to feed her babies. st. In two or three can fly! gbird seems very piderwebs let the nest babies grow! I like bird because it is l, and amazing.

Publish ▶ **Share your final copy.**

Creating a Title

Adding a title helps you introduce the report to your readers.

Tori wrote three different titles. She chose her favorite one and starred it.

1. **Name your topic.**

   Hummingbirds

2. **Describe your topic.**

   Tiny, Shiny Birds

3. **Be creative.**

   Humming Wonders *

Publish ▶ **Create a title.**

1. Try the three ways above to write a title.
2. Choose your favorite one.

Multimedia Presentation

Have you ever seen a slide show on a computer? Tori decided to turn her report into a slide show. It was a fun way to share her ideas.

You can make a slide show with your report, too. This chapter will show you how.

Prewriting ▶ Planning Your Slide Show

Plan your slide show carefully and gather a lot of ideas.

Tori made a slide grid. She wrote the main ideas for each slide. She added ideas for pictures, sounds, and actions.

Slide Grid

main ideas	pictures	sounds	actions
1. Humming Wonders (title)	hummingbird by flower	humming	flying bird
2. Birds are tiny and shiny. (paragraph 1)	big picture of a hummingbird	louder humming	bird flying in different directions
3. Humming birds eat	bird with beak in flower	humming	bird hovering

Prewrite ▶ **Plan your slide show.**

1. Make your own slide grid.
2. Write the main idea for each slide.
3. Add ideas for pictures, sounds, and actions.

Prewriting ▶ Making Your Storyboard

Next, you should make a storyboard for your presentation.

Tori made this storyboard.
She used her grid for ideas.

Part of Storyboard

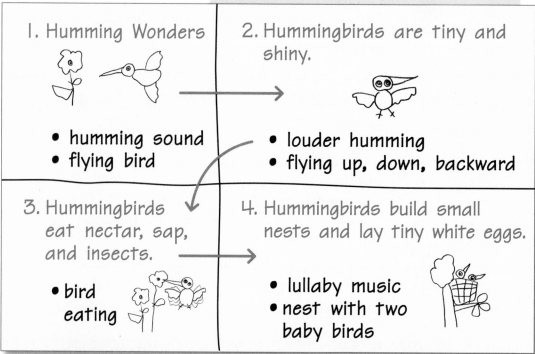

Prewrite ▶ Create your storyboard.

1. Create each slide using your grid as a guide.
2. Write the main ideas, pictures, sounds, and actions for each slide.

Write ▶ Create your slides.

1. Make an index card for each slide. Write what you will say while showing each slide.
2. Use a computer program to make your slides. Include pictures and sounds.

Revise ▶ Improve your presentation.

3. Did you include all the important ideas?
4. Did you put the slides in the right order?

Edit ▶ Check for conventions.

5. Did you spell words correctly?
6. Did you capitalize names and the first words of sentences?
7. Did you use end punctuation?

Publish ▶ Share your slide show.

8. Practice reading and showing your computer slides.
9. Give your presentation in class or at home.

The Tools of Learning

Writing Focus

- Giving Speeches
- Journals and Learning Logs
- Viewing and Listening Skills
- Taking Tests

Academic Vocabulary

Work with a partner. Read the meanings and share your answers.

1. A speech is a talk in front of an audience.
   Tell about a speech you have heard.

2. Your purpose for doing something is your reason for doing it.
   What is your purpose for brushing your teeth?

3. A visual aid is a picture or video used to help people learn.
   What is a visual aid that your teacher has used?

Dr. Martin Luther King, Jr., gave many great speeches. His most famous one is the "I Have a Dream" speech. People who listened to this speech never forgot it.

In this section, you will learn about making your own speeches. You will also learn about other skills that will make you a better student.

Giving Speeches

Do you have a collection? Do you know how to make something? Have you just learned about an interesting topic?

You can share your special information in a classroom speech. Paco's speech about fool's gold is on the next page. After reading his speech, you will learn how to prepare your own.

Paco's Speech

Fool's Gold

When my family went to Colorado to visit my uncle, he gave me this rock. It's called pyrite. It's also called fool's gold.

Pyrite is shiny like real gold, but it is made of iron and sulfur. Pyrite is harder than gold. It makes sparks if you hit it. That's how it got its name. Pyrite means fire. Sometimes pyrite is made into jewelry. It's not as valuable as gold because it's easy to find.

Pyrite might be fool's gold, but it has real value to me. It's my favorite rock in my rock collection.

Prewriting ▶ Choosing a Topic

To choose a topic, you first need to know why you are giving a speech. This is called "knowing your purpose."

Paco knew his purpose was to give information. He tried these three ways to choose an informational topic.

> 1. **Tell about something you like to do.**
>
>   I like to go fishing.

> 2. **Tell about something you learned.**
>
>   I learned about Ruby Bridges.

> 3. **Change a report you wrote into a speech.**
>
>   My report about fool's gold could make an interesting speech.

Prewrite ▶ **Choose your topic.**

1. Know your purpose.
2. Try different ways to choose a topic.

Gathering Details

After you select a topic, gather details for your speech. You can turn a report into a speech, or you can make a speech about a new topic.

Paco decided to turn his report on fool's gold into a speech. He reread the report and gathered important details to include in his speech.

Organizing Your Details

Next, organize the details for your speech.

Paco listed details for each part of his speech.

Beginning	Name your topic and get the listeners' attention.
Middle	Share the main facts about the topic.
Ending	Tell why the topic is important.

Prewrite ▶ **Gather and organize details.**

1. Gather details about your topic.
2. Plan the main parts of your speech.

Writing ▸ Preparing Your Speech

You can write your speech out word for word, or you may prepare it on note cards.

Paco looked at his details and wrote his speech on note cards.

Beginning

Name your subject.

> 1.
> When I went to Colorado to visit my uncle, he gave me this rock. It's called pyrite, or fool's gold.

Middle

List main facts about your subject.

> 2.
> - Shiny like gold, but not as valuable
> - Hard, makes sparks if hit
> - "Pyrite" means fire
> - Sometimes made into jewelry

Ending

Tell why the subject is important.

> 3.
> Pyrite might be fool's gold, but it has real value to me. It is my favorite rock in my rock collection.

Write ▸ **Prepare your speech.**

1. Look over your details and your plan.
2. Make note cards like those above. (Or write out your speech word for word.)

Publishing ▶ Giving Your Speech

Before you give your speech, you should practice it many times. (See the tips below.) It is easier to give a good speech once you know it well.

Paco practiced his speech for his family. When he gave his speech in school, he was careful to speak slowly, clearly, and loudly. He also tried to relax and enjoy himself.

Practice Tips

Use your note cards or paper as you practice your speech.

Share any visual aid you have.

Say your speech again and again until you know it by heart.

Publish ▶ Give your speech.

1. Look at your audience.
2. Speak slowly, clearly, and loudly.
3. Relax, smile, and enjoy giving your speech.

Writing in
Journals and Learning Logs

Most authors keep **journals** for writing down things. Keeping a journal gives them ideas for writing.

This chapter will show you how to keep your own journal. It will also tell you about learning logs.

Keeping a Personal Journal

A **personal journal** is your own special writing place. You can write about things that happen to you and things you wonder about.

Miki went on a field trip with her class. She wrote about it in her journal.

Miki's Journal Entry

January 19, 2011

My class went to the Garden Domes. It felt like summer inside the domes. The flowers were pretty. The air smelled sweet. There were birds singing and flying around everywhere! I think I'll dream about summer tonight.

practice

1. Start your personal journal.
2. Write the date at the top of the page.
3. Tell about what you did or what happened.

Writing in a Reading Journal

A reading journal is a place to write about the books you read. When you write, you can answer these types of questions:

- How do I feel about this book or story?
- What is my favorite part?
- Who is my favorite character?
- What did I learn from this book?

In this journal, Jamal told how he feels about a folktale he read.

Jamal's Journal Entry

March 31, 2011

The drawings in The Paper Crane are really cool. The story is about folded paper cranes. I want to make cranes out of paper, too.

practice

Write a journal entry about a book you have read.

Writing in a Learning Log

In a learning log, you write about what you learn in class. It helps you understand new ideas.

Katie wrote about what she learned in her science class.

Katie's Learning-Log Entry

September 22, 2011

Today we experimented with compasses. We learned that a compass has a magnet inside that points north. That's because the North Pole has a magnetic pull.

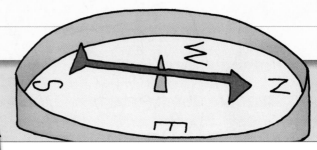

practice

Write a learning-log entry about something you learned in science. Draw a picture, too.

Viewing and Listening Skills

You can learn a lot just by watching and listening in class and at home.

This chapter will help you be a smart viewer of TV programs, commercials, and Web sites. It will also teach you how to be a good listener.

Viewing News Programs

News programs report important information about what is happening in your community, across the country, and around the world. A **news story** answers the 5 W questions about an event.

Jacob watched a news story and then answered the 5 W's.

Sample News Story

Who?	a wheelchair basketball team
What?	played a game
Where?	at the high school
When?	Saturday afternoon
Why?	to raise money for the team

Talk it over.

1. Watch a news story with an adult.
2. Listen for answers to the 5 W's.
3. Afterward, talk about the story. Did it answer all the questions?

Viewing TV Programs

TV programs can be about almost anything. They can be fun and interesting to watch.

Raul watched a program about talking drums. Raul did several things to make the viewing more interesting.

Before Viewing Raul wrote questions about the subject of the program.

During Viewing During the program, Raul listed answers to his questions.

After Viewing After Raul watched the program, he wrote about it to help him remember what he learned. He shared the main ideas and drew a picture.

Raul's Notes and Response

Questions	Answers
What are talking drums?	drums with long strings
Where do people use them?	Africa
Why do people use them?	send messages

November 11

    I watched a TV show about talking drums. People in Ghana, Africa, use these drums. Drummers send messages to each other. They make high and low sounds by pulling the drum's strings. The sounds stand for different words and feelings. The messages tell about being happy, excited, or scared. This is what the drum looks like.

practice

1. Choose a TV program to watch.
2. Ask questions about the topic. List answers during the show.
3. Write about the program.

Understanding Commercials

TV commercials are made to get your attention. Most of them try to get you to buy something. You need to use your best viewing and listening skills to understand what they are trying to do.

Two Selling Methods

Here are two ways commercials try to get you to buy something.

Be just like a famous person.

Melinda Lou is a champion swimmer because she takes a Swifty vitamin every day. You should take Swifty vitamins, too.

Join the crowd.

Everyone is buying the newest Super Duper Scooter. Hurry! Buy one now while supplies last.

Talk it over.

Do you know about any commercials that use these selling methods? Talk about them with your classmates.

Viewing Web Sites

Web sites can link you to people and places all over the world. These sites help you learn about any topic. Follow the tips below to find good information on the Web.

Web Surfing

Ask   Ask your parents, your teacher, or the librarian for help.

Look   Look up Web sites that end in **.org**, **.gov**, or **.edu**.

Learn Learn about the same topic on at least two sites. Then compare the facts.

practice

1. As a class, pick a topic to learn about.
2. Find two Web sites about the topic.
3. Compare the facts on the two sites.

Learning to Listen

How is hearing different from listening? You hear things like a school bell and a car horn. You listen to a friend's story or your teacher's directions. Hearing doesn't take a lot of thinking, but listening does.

Hearing

Hearing is knowing there are sounds all around you.

Your brother talking

The TV in the next room

Piano music

The checklist on the next page will show you how to be a good listener. When you are a good listener, you learn a lot more.

Listening

Listening takes more work than simple hearing. You must think about the sounds and sights around you.

Your brother
sharing a story

A TV special you
are watching

Your piano teacher
demonstrating a new melody

Did you check?

✓ 1. Look at the speaker.

✓ 2. Listen for key words like *first*, *most important, last,* and so on.

✓ 3. Ask questions when the person stops talking.

✓ 4. Write down the main ideas to help you remember them.

Taking Tests

In school you learn new things and practice new skills. You make things. Then you sometimes take tests!

Tests are important because they help you and your teacher know if you understand what you are studying.

Here are some tips to follow when you take a test.

Test-Taking Tips

Write your name on the top of your paper.

Listen to all the directions your teacher gives.

Ask questions if you do not understand something.

Answer the questions you are sure of first.

Skip the ones you are not sure of.

Return and answer any questions you skipped.

Check all your answers.

Multiple-Choice Test

In a **multiple-choice test**, you may have a list of sentences to complete. Your job is to pick the best choice to complete each sentence. Here are some tips.

Read	Read the sentence using each choice.
Reread	Then reread the sentence with your best choice.
Be Sure	Be sure your choice makes sense.

Sample

Directions: Fill in the circle in front of the word that best completes each sentence.

1. Bats are the only mammal that can _____.
   Ⓐ eat insects   Ⓑ make sounds   Ⓒ fly

2. The smallest bats are _____.
   Ⓐ six inches long   Ⓑ an inch long
   Ⓒ one foot long

3. _____ are the greatest threat to bats.
   Ⓐ People   Ⓑ Snakes   Ⓒ Bears

Answers: 1. Ⓒ   2. Ⓑ   3. Ⓐ

Matching Test

A **matching test** has two lists of words. You must match each word in the first list with a word in the second list. Here are some tips.

Start   Start with the first word in the left column.

Read   Read the words in the right column to find a word that matches.

Make   Make neat lines to match the words.

Sample

Directions: Draw a line from each word in column A to the word with the opposite meaning in column B.

A	B
1. dark	soft
2. sharp	light
3. hard	dull

Answers: 1. dark–light 2. sharp–dull 3. hard–soft

Fill-in-the-Blanks Test

A **fill-in-the-blanks** test gives you a list of sentences to complete. You write the correct word or words on the blanks. Here are some tips.

Read	Read each sentence carefully.
Choose	Choose a word from the word bank.
Read	Read the sentence with the word in it. (Be sure the word makes sense before you write it.)

Sample

Directions: Look at the picture and read each sentence. Then find a word in the word bank to complete each sentence. Write the word on the line.

Word Bank

> gas   liquid   solid

1. Hot chocolate is a _____.

2. The hot chocolate's steam is a _____.

3. The mug is a _____.

Answers: 1. liquid 2. gas 3. solid

Short-Answer Test

In a **short-answer test**, you write answers in complete sentences. Here are two tips.

Read	Read each question carefully.
Answer	Answer the question in one or two complete sentences.

Sample

Directions: Write complete sentences to answer each of the following questions.

1. Who lives in the White House?

   The president of the United

   States lives in the White House.

2. What does the American flag look like?

   The American flag has red and

   white stripes. It also has a blue

   box with 50 white stars inside.

Basic Grammar and Writing

What's Ahead

Academic Vocabulary

Work with a partner. Read the meanings and share your answers.

1. A sentence is a group of words that expresses a complete thought.
   What are some parts of a sentence?

2. When you practice, you do something over and over again until you are good at it.
   What is something that you practice?

3. Something is general if it is not special.
   Which word is more general, *flower* or *rose*?

Do you remember playing with blocks? Maybe you liked building forts or houses or towers. Words are just like building blocks, but instead of places, you build sentences. This section will help you use the best words in your sentences.

Working with Words

You already know many, many words, and you will learn many more as you read and study.

Words fit into different groups. Some words are nouns, some are pronouns, and so on. This chapter talks about nouns, pronouns, verbs, adjectives, and adverbs.

What's Ahead

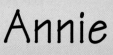

Learning About Nouns

A **noun** is a word that names a **person**, **place**, or **thing**.

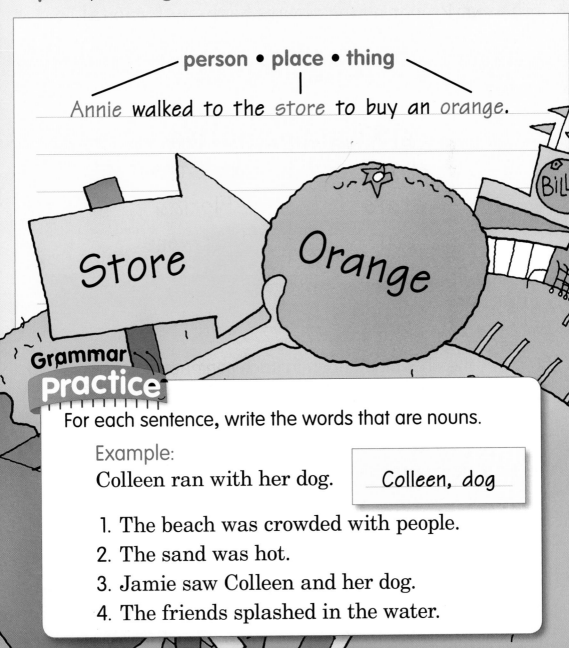

person • place • thing

Annie walked to the store to buy an orange.

Store

Orange

BILL'S

Grammar practice

For each sentence, write the words that are nouns.

Example:

Colleen ran with her dog. | Colleen, dog

1. The beach was crowded with people.
2. The sand was hot.
3. Jamie saw Colleen and her dog.
4. The friends splashed in the water.

Common and Proper Nouns

A **common noun** names any person, place, or thing. A **proper noun** names a special person, place, or thing. Proper nouns always begin with capital letters.

Common Nouns	Proper Nouns
girl	Lina
street	Oak Street
state	Florida
cat	Whiskers

Grammar practice

Copy the underlined noun in each sentence below. Write **P** if it is a proper noun. Write **C** if it is a common noun. Capitalize the proper nouns.

Example:

I flew with Mom to sun valley.　　Sun Valley, P

1. My cousin, thomas, lives there.
2. He plays the violin.
3. I played with his dog, bowser.
4. My cousin is coming here to visit.

Singular and Plural Nouns

Nouns can be singular or plural. **Singular** means *one*. **Plural** means *more than one*. To make most nouns plural, add **-s** at the end of the word.

Singular Nouns	Plural Nouns
coat	coats
rabbit	rabbits
girl	girls

Grammar practice

Copy the underlined noun in each sentence below. Write **S** if the noun is singular and **PL** if it is plural.

Example:

Mike and Andi opened their <u>eyes</u>.

eyes, PL

1. They saw two new <u>bikes</u>.
2. Andi put on her <u>jacket</u>.
3. Mike quickly put on his <u>shoes</u>.
4. The twins took a <u>ride</u>.

Nouns That End in -es

To form the plural of a noun that ends with **sh**, **ch**, **x**, **s**, and **z**, add **-es** to the end of the word.

Singular Nouns	Plural Nouns
wish	wishes
bunch	bunches
box	boxes
dress	dresses
buzz	buzzes

Grammar practice

Write the plural form for the underlined noun in each sentence below.

Example:

Mom set all the <u>dish</u> on the table.   dishes

1. Dad made several <u>batch</u> of pancakes.
2. Grandma used two <u>mix</u> for the dip.
3. Gina picked <u>bunch</u> of violets.
4. Mom put them in tall <u>glass</u> on the table.

Nouns That End in y

To form the plural of many nouns that end in **y**, remember this rule.

> Change the **y** to **i** and add **-es**.

$$\text{lady} \longrightarrow \text{ladi} + es = \text{ladies}$$

Singular Nouns	Plural Nouns
puppy	puppies
penny	pennies
jelly	jellies
story	stories

Grammar practice

Use the rule above to write the plural of each noun below. Then use each plural noun in a sentence.

Example:
country

> countries
>
> Dad travels to many countries.

1. party   2. pony   3. baby   4. city

Possessive Nouns

A **possessive noun** shows ownership. To make a singular noun possessive, place an **'s** at the end of the word. To form most plural possessives, add the apostrophe (**'**) at the end of the word.

Have you seen Bobbi's hamster?

> The hamster belongs to Bobbi.

We saw the rabbits' tracks.

> The tracks belong to more than one rabbit.

Grammar practice

For each sentence, write the possessive noun.

Example:

Our neighbor's car is orange. | neighbor's |

1. Mr. Lee's dog is friendly.
2. That bicycle's tire is flat.
3. The school's doors were just painted.
4. The boys' softball gloves got wet.

How can I use nouns?

Use **specific nouns** to give the reader a better picture of what you mean. If you use the word *flower*, it means any flower. But if you use the word *tulip*, your reader knows exactly what you mean.

General Nouns	Clear Nouns
neighbor	Mr. Cosfa
park	Central Park
building	firehouse
dog	terrier
tree	maple

Grammar practice

For each general noun below, write a clear noun.

Example:
teacher   Ms. Daniels

1. show
2. friend
3. store
4. bird
5. snack

Using Pronouns

A **pronoun** is a word that takes the place of a noun. Here are some common pronouns.

I	he	she	we	they	you
me	him	her	us	them	it

Then Claudia and Stella jumped rope.

Look at how the pronoun they replaces the nouns in the sentence above.

Then they jumped rope.

Grammar practice

For each sentence, write the pronoun.

Example:
She will walk the dog. **She**

1. They see a deer cross the road.
2. "Does the deer see us?" asked Sam.
3. Then the deer sees them.
4. The dog barks at it, and the deer runs.

Singular and Plural Pronouns

Pronouns are **singular** and **plural** just like nouns. Remember that singular means *one* and plural means *more than one*.

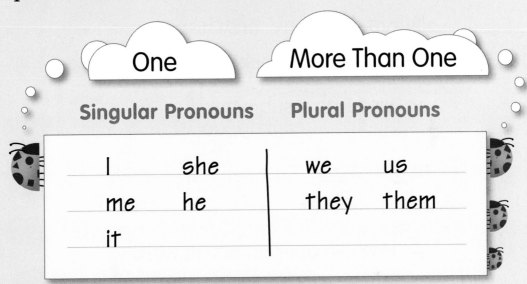

One   More Than One

Singular Pronouns   Plural Pronouns

I	she	we	us
me	he	they	them
it			

Grammar practice

Choose the correct pronoun to take the place of the underlined noun or nouns.

Example:

Susan smiled. *(She, They)*   She

1. Hanna and Kim play. *(He, They)*
2. The bird flew to the feeder. *(We, It)*
3. Where was Franco? *(he, they)*
4. Theresa swims well. *(She, He)*

Using *I* and *Me*

When you write about yourself, use the singular pronoun **I** or **me**. The word **I** is always capitalized.

I always help my brother.
Tam and I are working together.

> Use I as a subject.

Fran gave me the letter.
Sandi told Mom and me about it.

> Use **me** after an action verb.

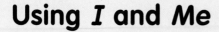

Grammar practice

Choose the correct pronoun for each sentence.

Example:
Lori asked (*I, me*) to go skating. | me

1. (*I, me*) ran around the playground.
2. Jack and (*I, me*) played tag.
3. Dad asked (*I, me*) to clean my room.
4. Tom told Mom and (*I, me*) about the trip.

Using *We* and *Us*

When you write about yourself and others, use the plural pronouns **we** and **us**.

We are going to the school picnic.

> Use **we** as the **subject** of a sentence.

Mr. Tylor asked us a few questions.

> Use **us** after an action verb.

Grammar practice

Choose either **we** or **us** for each sentence below.

Example:
Please give _____ the invitations.

> us

1. _____ will plan the party together.
2. Mom and Dad always give _____ snacks.
3. _____ want to make the decorations.
4. Please tell _____ what to do next.

Possessive Pronouns

A **possessive pronoun** shows who or what owns something. It takes the place of a possessive noun.

| my | his | her | its | our | their |

Possessive Nouns	Possessive Pronouns
Devon's mitt	his mitt
Jenna's class	her class
Tom and Bina's pictures	their pictures
the book's cover	its cover

Grammar practice

Choose the correct pronoun for each underlined possessive noun below.

Example:

That is <u>Dee and Jen's</u> house. *(their, her)* their

1. Did you find <u>Olivia's</u> locket? *(her, its)*
2. Mom saw <u>Leon's</u> hat. *(her, his)*
3. This is <u>Jake and Ron's</u> room. *(their, his)*
4. We fixed the <u>bike's</u> tire. *(its, his)*

How can I use pronouns?

Pronouns can be used to form contractions. A **contraction** is a shortened word made from two words.

Pronoun + Verb = Contraction

he	+ is	=	he's
she	+ is	=	she's
it	+ is	=	it's
you	+ are	=	you're
we	+ are	=	we're
they	+ are	=	they're

> An apostrophe (') shows that one or more letters are left out.

Grammar practice

Write the contraction for each set of words in the sentences below.

Example:
(They are) planting a garden.   They're

1. I think *(it is)* almost time to go home.
2. Coach Lee says *(you are)* a good pitcher.
3. *(He is)* our neighbor.
4. Mom said *(we are)* going on a trip!

Learning About Verbs

There are three main types of verbs: action verbs, helping verbs, and linking verbs.

Action Verbs

An **action verb** tells what action is being done.

The kangaroo hops.

My puppy jumps.

Our friend Lin sings.

Grammar practice

Write the action verb from each sentence below.

Example:

We clean our desks. | clean |

1. The rain pounds the sidewalk.
2. Little frogs leap in the grass.
3. The trees bend in the wind.
4. We hear thunder.
5. I love summer storms.

Helping Verbs

Helping verbs come before the main verb. They help to show action or time. Here are some examples.

am	is	are	was	were	will

We were reading stories.

The helping verb **were** helps the main verb **reading**.

Grammar practice

Write the helping verb and the main verb from each sentence below.

Example:

I am playing at Katie's house.   am playing

1. We were making a scrapbook.
2. I am finding pictures for the pages.
3. Katie was looking for decorations.
4. She is collecting buttons and ribbons.
5. Katie and I will use markers and crayons.

Linking Verbs

Linking verbs complete a thought by linking two ideas in a sentence. The follow *be* verbs can be linking verbs. (Most linking verbs can also be used as helping verbs. See page 341.)

> am   is   are   was   were

I am hungry.

My cat is very pretty.

Sam and Dana are friends.

Lani was a funny girl.

We were lost.

Grammar practice

Write a sentence for each of the linking verbs below. Underline the linking verbs in your sentences.

Example:
were

We <u>were</u> late for school.

1. am   3. are   5. were
2. is   4. was

Verb Tenses

The tense of a verb tells when the action happens. The action can happen in the **present**, in the **past**, or in the **future**.

Present Tense The action is happening.

Andy skates with his friends.

Past Tense The action did happen.

Andy skated yesterday.

Future Tense The action will happen.

Andy will skate tomorrow.

Grammar practice

Write a sentence for each of the verbs below. Then tell the tense of each verb.

Example:
visited

Owen visited the Grand Canyon last year. past tense

1. plays
2. will bake
3. dropped
4. reads
5. talked

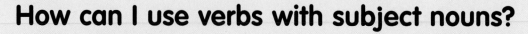

How can I use verbs with subject nouns?

A verb will be correct if it **agrees in number** with its subject noun. That means a singular subject needs a singular verb, and a plural subject needs a plural verb.

Singular Subject Noun	Singular Verb
Juan	laughs.
Dad	cleans.
Sue	dives.

Plural Subject Noun	Plural Verb
The boys	laugh.
We	clean.
Kim and I	dive.

Grammar practice

For each sentence below, write the verb that agrees with the subject.

Example:

Lucy (*play, plays*) in the band. | plays

1. The children (*draw, draws*) pictures.
2. Gabe (*buy, buys*) a comic book.
3. Jon (*ride, rides*) his bike after school.
4. My friends (*play, plays*) chess.

How can I use verbs correctly with subject pronouns?

Your verb will be correct if it **agrees in number** with its subject pronoun. Look at the chart below.

Singular Subject Pronoun	Singular Verb	Plural Subject Pronoun	Plural Verb
He	likes snow.	They	like snow.
She	wants help.	We	want help.
It	drinks water.	They	drink water.

Grammar practice

For each sentence below, write the verb that agrees with the subject.

Example:

We (go, goes) to the park.   go

1. They (find, finds) a lost dog.
2. It (wag, wags) its tail!
3. She (want, wants) to find the owners.
4. They (make, makes) a lost-and-found poster.
5. He (is, are) happy to see Spot again.

Working with Adjectives

An **adjective** is a word that describes a noun. Adjectives help you add details to your writing.

Adjectives tell what kind.

Adjectives that tell **what kind** make writing fun to read.

> The huge owl flew away.
> The dog chased the yellow ball.

Grammar practice

For each sentence below, find the adjective that tells what kind.

Example:
Let's visit the brick building.   brick

1. The building has a round dome.
2. A squeaky fan cools me.
3. I ate a spicy burrito.
4. My old quilt comforts me.
5. We played in the white sand.

Adjectives tell which one.

Adjectives that tell **which one** make your writing clear. Here are some examples.

> this   that   those   these

This book is very exciting.

I want to read that book again.

Did you hear those stories?

These pictures are my favorite.

Grammar practice

For each sentence below, find the adjective that tells which one.

Example:

This book shows men on the moon. | This |

1. Grandpa remembers that day.
2. Those astronauts were brave.
3. Grandpa gave me these pictures.
4. This photo shows the moon.
5. Just look at those craters!

Adjectives tell how many.

Some adjectives tell you **how many**.

one **tree**	three **tickets**
two **pages**	four **birds**

Grammar practice

Write a sentence for each adjective below.

Example:
one

Winslow School has one gym.

1. two   2. three   3. four   4. five

Articles

A, *an*, and *the* are special adjectives called **articles**. Use *a* before words that begin with a consonant. Use *an* before words that begin with a vowel.

a **lamb**	an **octopus**	the **zoo**

Grammar practice

Write one sentence using **a**, one sentence using **an**, and one sentence using **the**.

How can I use adjectives?

You can use adjectives to **compare** two people, places, or things.

Our car is smaller than your car.

> To compare **two** nouns, add **-er** to the end of the adjective.

The red car is the smallest one of all.

> To compare **three** or *more* nouns, add **-est** to the end of the adjective.

Grammar practice

In each sentence below, choose the correct adjective.

Example:

I am (*older, oldest*) than Tim.   older

1. He is the (*younger, youngest*) boy in class.
2. Danni is a (*faster, fastest*) runner than I am.
3. She is the (*taller, tallest*) girl I know.
4. Your chair is (*softer, softest*) than mine.

Learning About Adverbs

An **adverb** is a word that describes a verb. It answers **when**, **where**, or **how** an action happens.

It rained yesterday. (When?)

We ran inside. (Where?)

The thunder rumbled loudly. (How?)

Grammar practice

For each sentence below, write the adverb that answers the asking word in parentheses.

Example:

Mom and I went fishing today. (When?)

today

1. We sat quietly. (How?)
2. The fish swam quickly. (How?)
3. I let my bait sink down. (Where?)
4. A bluegill finally grabbed the bait. (When?)
5. I carefully put the fish back. (How?)

How can I use adverbs?

Using adverbs helps to make your writing clear. The adverbs in the following sentences answer **how**.

How?

Roy slowly poured the water.

Maria proudly read her report.

The snow fell softly.

Grammar practice

Write each sentence below, using the adverb in parentheses that you like best.

Example:

The snake slithered *(silently, quickly)*.

> The snake slithered silently.

1. Otters swim *(smoothly, gracefully)*.
2. Prairie dogs *(quickly, always)* pop out of their holes.
3. Monkeys *(carefully, cleverly)* peel bananas.
4. Woodpeckers *(noisily, nervously)* peck trees.

Building
Sentences

Sentences come in all sizes. Some are very long. Others are quite short. Every sentence must tell a complete thought. It must also begin with a capital letter and end with a punctuation mark. In this chapter, you will learn all about sentences.

What's Ahead

Writing Complete Sentences

Correct Word Order

The words in a sentence must be in the correct order to make sense. The first group of words below does not make sense.

hamburger Billy eats a lunch for

If you put these words in the correct order, they tell a complete, clear sentence.

Billy eats a hamburger for lunch.

Grammar practice

Put the groups of words below in the correct order to make sentences.

Example:

is hamburger the hot.   The hamburger is hot.

1. pickles puts hamburger on his Billy
2. squirts his on ketchup hamburger he
3. a little likes also he mustard

Subject of a Sentence

The **naming part** of a sentence is called the **subject**. The subject tells who or what the sentence is about.

Ms. Davis is our teacher.

She walks to school.

Ms. Davis is the **subject** of the first sentence. **She** is the **subject** of the second sentence.

Grammar
practice

Write the subject of each sentence below.

Example:
The school is near our teacher's house.

> The school

1. The house has a big porch.
2. Students walk past her house.
3. Parents wave to Ms. Davis.
4. The crossing guard helps the students.
5. Students carry the teacher's book bag.

Predicate of a Sentence

The **telling part** of a sentence is called the **predicate**. It tells what the subject does. The predicate always includes a main verb.

Crickets *chirp loudly.*

Chirp loudly is the predicate. It tells what the crickets do. The word **chirp** is the main verb.

Grammar practice

Write the predicate of each sentence below.

Example:
Crickets look like grasshoppers.

look like grasshoppers

1. Many crickets hide during the day.
2. Crickets live on trees.
3. They move slowly in cold weather.
4. Field crickets eat grass and wood.
5. Some people keep crickets as pets.

Fixing Sentence Problems

Sentence Fragments

Every sentence needs a subject and a predicate to make sense. A **sentence fragment** is missing a subject or a predicate (verb).

Fragments	Sentences
Sleeps under a tree. (A subject is missing.)	The dog sleeps under a tree. (A subject is added.)
The dog in the yard. (A verb is missing.)	The dog runs in the yard. (A verb is added.)

Grammar practice

The sentence fragments below are missing a subject or a verb. Make each one a sentence.

Example:
Ranger loudly. | Ranger barks loudly.

1. plays in the park.
2. Ranger into the pond.
3. Chased me.
4. Water all over.

Rambling Sentences

A **rambling sentence** is one that goes on and on and on.

Rambling Sentences

My mother told me to get some skim milk and I went to the cooler and I looked for a carton and I finally found it.

Try not to use the word **and** too many times.

Better Sentences

My mother told me to get some skim milk. I went to the cooler and looked for a carton. I finally found it.

Grammar practice

Rewrite this rambling sentence. Turn it into three or four sentences by taking out some of the *and's*.

Joanie calls her friends and she asks them to go to the park and they have fun swinging and they have fun sliding.

Subject-Verb Agreement

Subjects and verbs must agree in number. A singular subject must have a singular verb. A plural subject must have a plural verb.

Bob has a silver wheelchair.

> The **subject** and the **verb** are singular.

Two other boys have red wheelchairs.

> The **subject** and the **verb** are plural.

Grammar practice

Write the verb that agrees with the subject for each sentence below.

Example:
Bob (*go, goes*) to Cooper School. | *goes*

1. Justin (*push, pushes*) Bob's wheelchair.
2. Justin and Bob (*is, are*) good friends.
3. Bob (*tell, tells*) funny stories.
4. His friends always (*laugh, laughs*).

Using Different Kinds of Sentences

A **telling sentence** makes a statement.

You have a box of crayons.

An **asking sentence** asks a question.

Do you have a red crayon?

A **command sentence** gives directions or makes a request.

Put your crayons away.

An **exclamatory sentence** shows surprise or strong feelings.

Your crayons are going to fall!

Grammar practice

Write what kind of sentence each one is.

Example:

Crayons are made in many colors.   telling

1. How many crayons do you have?
2. I love your drawing!
3. Pass me the blue crayon.
4. I want to draw the ocean.

Combining Short Sentences

Sometimes, short sentences have the same subject. These sentences can be combined to make longer sentences.

Short Sentences with the Same Subject

Jerry gets dressed. Jerry eats breakfast.

Combined Sentences

Jerry gets dressed and eats breakfast.

Grammar practice

Combine these sentences to make longer sentences.

Example:
The store buys fresh peaches.
The store sells fresh peaches.

The store buys and sells fresh peaches.

1. The school bus stops.
   The school bus picks up three students.
2. Jenna's friends talk. Jenna's friends laugh.
3. Kenny sits at his desk. Kenny opens his book.

You can also combine short sentences that have the same predicate.

Short Sentences with the Same Predicate

Ellen cleaned the board.

Lila cleaned the board.

Combined Sentences

Ellen and Lila cleaned the board.

Grammar practice

Combine these short sentences to make longer sentences. (You may need to change a singular verb to a plural verb in your new sentence.)

Example:

Sam reads a lot. Paula reads a lot.

Sam and Paula read a lot.

1. Sharon jumps rope during recess.
   Jill jumps rope during recess.
2. Ryan learns about question marks.
   Thomas learns about question marks.
3. The girls like the goldfish.
   The boys like the goldfish.

Practice Test

On your own paper,
write the letter that answers
each question.

1. Which sentence is a fragment?

Ⓐ The movie lasts two hours.
Ⓑ Bryan all the way home.
Ⓒ It is time for lunch.

2. Which sentence puts the following group of words in the correct order?

old eight today is years Bobby

Ⓐ Today is eight years old Bobby.
Ⓑ Old today is eight years Bobby.
Ⓒ Bobby is eight years old today.

3. What is the subject of this sentence?

George looks at the stars.

Ⓐ the stars
Ⓑ looks
Ⓒ George

4. What is the predicate of this sentence?

Russell sets the table.

Ⓐ sets the table

Ⓑ sets the

Ⓒ Russell

5. What kind of sentence is this?

Do you have a favorite book?

Ⓐ a telling sentence

Ⓑ an asking sentence

Ⓒ an exclamatory sentence

6. Which choice correctly combines these two short sentences?

Barb plays soccer. Jo plays soccer.

Ⓐ Jo plays soccer. Barb plays soccer.

Barb plays soccer and Jo.

Ⓒ Barb and Jo play soccer.

7. Which choice correctly combines these two sentences?

Sean hits the ball. Sean runs to first base.

Ⓐ Sean hits and runs the ball to first base.

Ⓑ Sean hits the ball and runs to first base.

Ⓒ Sean runs to first base. Sean hits the ball.

Writing Paragraphs

A paragraph is a group of sentences about the same topic. In a paragraph, you can describe something, give information, or tell how to do a task. Theo's paragraph on the next page tells about a hot-air balloon.

What's Ahead

Theo's Paragraph

What I Saw

Topic Sentence

    I saw a big hot-air balloon that looked like my sister's knee socks. It had bright blue and yellow stripes. A big basket with a man inside it

Body Sentences

hung under the balloon. The man shot spurts of fire into the balloon. Whoosh, whoosh! The flames made a loud sound. I waved to the man, and

Closing Sentence

he waved back! It was the coolest thing I have ever seen.

A paragraph has three main parts.

- The **topic sentence** tells what the paragraph is about. It states the main idea.
- The **body sentences** describe the topic.
- The **closing sentence** adds one last thought.

Writing a Topic Sentence

The **topic sentence** names the topic or the main idea of the paragraph. Here are three ways to write a topic sentence.

1. **Asking a Question**

   Have you ever seen a hot-air balloon?

2. **Stating an Interesting Idea**

   Yesterday, a colorful hot-air balloon floated over my house.

3. **Making a Comparison**

   I saw a big hot-air balloon that looked like my sister's knee socks.

Talk it over.

Do you like Theo's choice for a topic sentence? Tell why or why not.

Writing Body Sentences

The **body sentences** of a paragraph share details about the topic. You can use details from a quick planning list to write the body sentences of your paragraph. Here's Theo's quick list.

Quick List

- blue and yellow stripes
- a big basket with a man in it
- fire shot into balloon
- a loud whoosh sound

Example Body Sentences

It had bright blue and yellow stripes.

A big basket with a man inside it hung under the balloon.

The man shot spurts of fire into the balloon.

Writing a Closing Sentence

A **closing sentence** says one last thing about your topic. Theo wrote his closing sentence in two different ways. Then he chose the one he liked best.

1. Restating the Main Idea

Seeing the hot-air balloon was fun.

2. Adding a Final Thought

It was the coolest thing I have ever seen.

1. Write another ending sentence for Theo's paragraph.
2. Now write your own paragraph.

Indenting Each Paragraph

You **indent** a paragraph because it starts a new idea. *Indenting* means to begin writing farther in from the margin.

Example of Indenting

> The lion came close to the edge of its cage. It looked right at me. The lion growled, "Grrr!"
>
> Suddenly, Dad called me.

Talk it over.

Look at the writing below. What is the new idea in the second paragraph?

> I learned to swim! At first I was afraid of the water. Soon I was brave enough to swim in the deep water. Now swimming is my favorite thing to do.
>
> My little brother is learning to swim. I am helping him, but he is still a little afraid of the water. Today we will go swimming. I like swimming with my brother.

WRITE SOURCE Online
www.hmheducation.com/writesource

A Writer's Resource

Academic Vocabulary

Work with a partner. Read the meanings and share answers to the questions.

1. A **topic** is a subject of writing or speaking.
What topics do you enjoy discussing?

2. A **graphic organizer** shows how words or ideas are connected.
What are kinds of graphic organizers?

3. You can write down things you do or learn in a **journal**.
What would you write about in a journal?

4. A **resource** is something that can be used to help you find information.
What resources have you used this week?

Sometimes you need help with your writing. Maybe you can't think of a good topic. Or maybe you aren't sure how to gather details. Whenever you get stuck, turn to these pages for ideas and help.

How can I find a good topic?

Keep a writer's notebook.

Good writing ideas are everywhere. Keep a list of ideas in a notebook. Someday you may use these ideas in a story, a letter, a report, or even in a poem.

Write about what is going on around you.

You may see something interesting right in your own backyard.

Sample Writer's Notebook

A big gray squirrel is sitting on a bird feeder. How did it get up there? A red bird wants to come to the feeder. That squirrel is scaring the birds and throwing seeds all over!

List topics in your notebook.

List interesting people, places, and things in your writer's notebook. Then look over your lists when you need writing ideas.

Sample Writer's Notebook

People	Places	Things
teacher	school	car
pilot	home	bike
doctor	Ohio	lion
parent	library	desk
brother	zoo	game

Finish sentence starters.

Your teachers may give you some sentence starters. You may also think of your own. Add them to your notebook.

Sample Writer's Notebook

I like to . . .
   I like to go fishing with Grandpa.
   I like to swing on tire swings!

I laugh when . . .
   I laugh when Cindy tells jokes.
   I laugh when my little brother makes faces.

Dogs bark because . . .
   Dogs bark because they like to talk, too!
   Dogs bark because they want to play.

Stormy days . . .
   Stormy days mean we have inside recess.
   Stormy days can be scary.

Keep a reading journal.

Read, read, read. Books and magazines are full of ideas. Keep a reading journal to write about what you learn in your reading.

Sample Reading-Journal Entry

March 18, 2012

Today I read about manatees.
They are also called sea cows.
They eat water plants just like
cows eat grass! They look as big
as a walrus and move very slowly.
Manatees live in Florida. Maybe I
can see them someday.

How can I find more writing ideas?

Use the basics-of-life words.

Basics-of-life words remind you of what people need to live.

Art	Community	Friends	Music
Animals	Family	Health	Shelter
Clothing	Food	Jobs	Weather

Sample Writing Idea (Shelter)

The word shelter makes me think of an igloo. I could write about how native people build igloos.

Sample Writing Idea (Friends)

The word friends makes me think of Erin and Sarah. I could write a story about making friends in my new school.

How can I find special topics?

Review lists of topic ideas.

For **descriptive** writing, you could **describe** . . .
- a sister, a cousin, an aunt, a teacher. (People)
- your room, the lunchroom, a library. (Places)
- a toy, a hat, a tree, an octopus. (Things)

For **narrative** writing, you could **tell what happened** . . .
- during a ride on the bus.
- on your first day of school.
- in a funny dream.

For **expository** writing, you could **explain** . . .
- how to fly a kite.
- how to draw funny faces.
- information about eagles.

For **persuasive** writing, you could **convince** your reader to . . .
- be polite on a field trip.
- eat a good breakfast.
- read a special book.

How do I write topic sentences?

Know your purpose.

You write to describe, to share a story, to explain, or to convince someone. The reason for your writing is called your **purpose**. A topic sentence lets the reader know the main idea and purpose of a paragraph.

To Describe
Descriptive writing helps the reader see or hear a topic.

The red race car sounds like a jet plane.

To Share a Story
Narrative writing tells a story.

Yesterday, my brother broke his arm.

To Explain Something
Expository writing shares information.

Giving a dog a bath is a big job.

To Convince Someone
Persuasive writing tries to get the reader to agree with an opinion.

A turtle makes a great pet.

How can I organize my ideas?

Use graphic organizers.

When you play softball, you follow a plan. First, you and your friends choose sides. Then you decide who bats first and so on. When you write, you also need a plan, and a graphic organizer can help. Look at the graphic organizer below and on pages 380–385.

List steps in a sequence chart.

Use a **sequence chart** to put details in order. Then follow the chart as you write.

Sequence Chart

Topic	How to Bake Bread
First	Find the ingredients.
Next	Mix the ingredients.
Then	Turn on the oven.
Last	Bake the ingredients.

Compare topics with a Venn diagram.

Use a **Venn diagram** when you compare two topics. In spaces 1 and 2, list how the topics are different. In space 3, list how the topics are alike.

Sample Venn Diagram

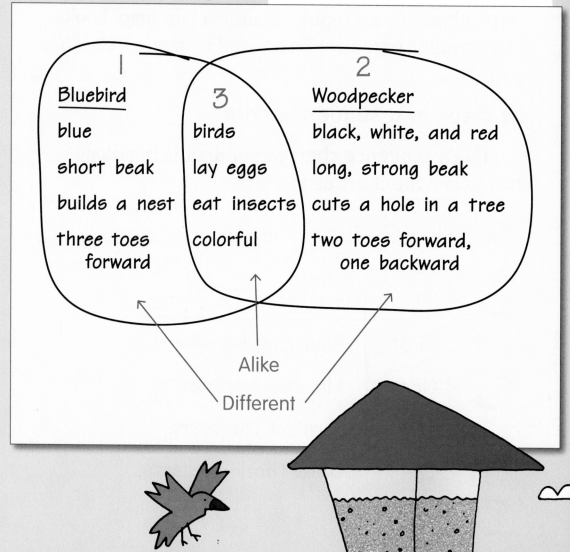

1 Bluebird	3	2 Woodpecker
blue	birds	black, white, and red
short beak	lay eggs	long, strong beak
builds a nest	eat insects	cuts a hole in a tree
three toes forward	colorful	two toes forward, one backward

Alike

Different

Gather details with a cluster.

Make a **cluster**, also called a **web**, about your topic. Write your topic in the middle of your paper. Draw a circle around it. Then write as many ideas as you can about your topic.

Sample Cluster

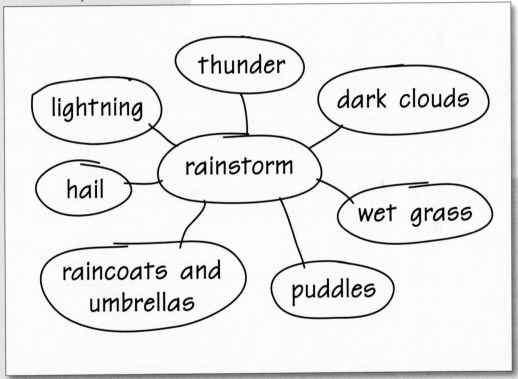

Gather details with a sensory chart.

Use a **sensory chart** to list different types of details for a topic.

Sensory Chart

Topic: Lunch

Sight	Sound	Smell	Taste	Touch
bowl of tomato soup	spoons clinking on bowls	tomatoes	tomatoes	hot bowl
		cooked corn	salty crackers	cool milk
square crackers	crunching			dry crackers
	laughter	toasted bread	sweet corn	
glass of milk				soft, gooey cheese
			melted cheese	
grilled cheese sandwich				hot corn
corn on the cob				

Plan a story with a map.

Use a **story map** to help you remember important parts of a story. You can draw pictures or write words to make a story map.

Story Map

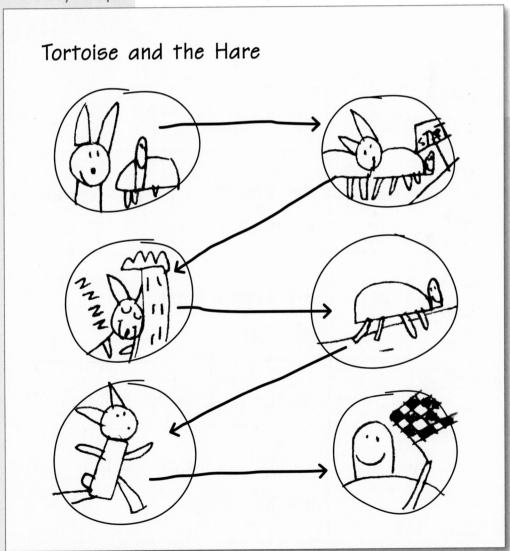

Tortoise and the Hare

Gather facts with a 5 W's chart.

Make a **5 W's chart** when you need to find important facts or details for your writing.

5 W's Chart

Who?	Mrs. Jones
What?	delivers the mail and small packages
When?	six days a week all year
Where?	to our apartment building
Why?	so we can read our mail it's her job

Put events in order with a time line.

Make a **time line** to show when different events happened. A time line can use hours, days, months, or years.

Sample Time Line

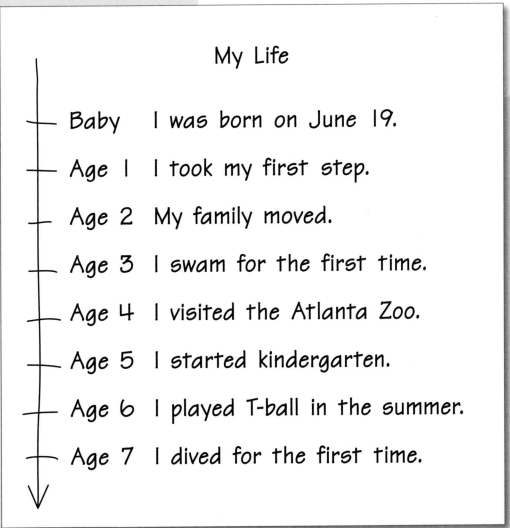

My Life

Baby   I was born on June 19.

Age 1   I took my first step.

Age 2   My family moved.

Age 3   I swam for the first time.

Age 4   I visited the Atlanta Zoo.

Age 5   I started kindergarten.

Age 6   I played T-ball in the summer.

Age 7   I dived for the first time.

How should my writing voice change?

Match your voice with your purpose.

Whenever you write, keep your purpose in mind. Be sure to sound interested and confident in your topic, too.

Descriptive Voice

Use sensory details to describe a topic.

> My dad's match hit the newspaper. Pretty soon smoke came up from the pile of sticks. Then yellow and orange flames licked the wood. Sparks jumped through the grill over our campfire.

Narrative Voice

Write as if you were telling the story to a friend.

> I had to take care of Felix for two weeks. If you knew Felix, you would say, "Good luck!" He is a big, stubborn cat who loves to hide.

Expository Voice

Use specific details to explain your topic. Help your reader to understand information or to follow the steps.

> First, you spread glue where you want the glitter on your drawing. Next, sprinkle the glitter on the glue. Let it dry for a minute. Then shake the extra glitter off. Finally, let your picture dry completely.

Persuasive Voice

Use good reasons to help the reader decide to agree with you.

> When you go outside on a very cold day, be sure to wear a hat. You lose a lot of heat from the top of your head. A hat helps to keep your whole body warm.

How can I learn new words?

Keep a new-word notebook.

Keep a notebook just for new words. Write each word and its meaning. Then write a sentence that uses that word. Add drawings if you wish.

New-Word Notebook

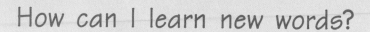

telescope (word)

an instrument used to look at stars (meaning)

Mara's family bought a telescope to look at the moon. (sentence)

tanker (word)

a truck or ship that carries liquids like water, milk, or oil (meaning)

The tanker pulled out of the gas station. (sentence)

Use a dictionary.

You can learn what a word means by looking it up in a dictionary.

Sample Dictionary Entry

> **insect** An insect is a small animal with six legs. A wasp is a flying insect. Some common insects are crickets, moths, and mosquitoes.

Sarah watches the red insect cross the sidewalk.

Use a thesaurus.

A **thesaurus** is a book that lists words and their synonyms (words with the same meanings). Use a thesaurus to choose specific words.

Sample Thesaurus Entry

> **jacket**   *noun* coat, parka, windbreaker

Word Choice

General ▶ Larry wore a jacket to the football game.

Specific ▶ Larry wore a parka to the football game.

How can I figure out a new word?

Use context clues.

Context clues are hints you find by reading the words all around a new word.

Read the words after the new word.

> The botanist studied plants in the rain forest.

> The words studied plants give you a clue about the meaning of the word botanist.

Look for words with the same meaning.

> The miniature poodle looked very small.

> The words very small mean the same thing as the word miniature.

Study pictures that show what a word means.

> The cowboy lassos the calf.

Divide the word into parts.

You can figure out the meaning of a new word by learning about *prefixes, roots,* and *suffixes.*

reviewer

The prefix **re** means again.

The root **view** means to look at carefully.

The suffix **er** means someone who does something.

A movie **reviewer** is someone who looks carefully again at a movie.

Learn prefixes.

A **prefix** is a word part that comes before the root. A prefix changes the meaning of the root word.

pre- (before)
pretest (before the final test)

re- (again)
rebuild (build something again)

un- (not)
unclear (not clear)

Learn suffixes.

A **suffix** is a word part that comes after a root word. A suffix changes the meaning of the root word.

-er, -or   (a person who does something)
coal miner   (a person who digs for coal)

-ful   (full)
playful   (full of play)

-ing   (doing something)
walking   (doing what it is to walk)

-less   (not having something)
sugarless   (having no sugar)

-ment   (act of)
government   (act of governing)

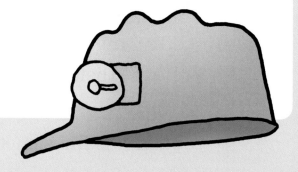

Remember root words.

The **root** is the main part of a word, without a prefix or a suffix. Study these roots.

cycl (wheel, circular)
   bicyc**le**   (a vehicle with two wheels)

fill (to make full)
   refill   (fill again)

flex (bend)
   flex**ible**   (able to bend)

graph   (write)
   autograph   (to write your own name)

mar (sea)
   submar**ine**   (an undersea ship)

meter (measure)
   thermometer   (an instrument that
                    measures temperature)

narr (tell)

    narrative (writing that tells a story)

photo (light)

    photograph (a picture formed by light)

port (carry)

    transportation (ways things are carried)

sphere (ball)

    spherical (shaped like a ball)

teach (teach)

    teacher (a person who teaches)

tele (far)

    telescope (an instrument for seeing things that are far away)

How can I connect my sentences?

Use time-order words.

Use **time-order words** to tell the order in which things happen or should be done.

Time-Order Word Chart

first	second	third
May 10	May 11	May 12
yesterday	today	tomorrow
then	now	later
first	next	last

Use place-order words.

Use **place-order words** to show location.

on top of · · · · **over, above**

beside, near

in

to the right of

outside

below, under

Place-Order Word Chart

above	**below**	**on top of**
across	**beneath**	**outside**
after	**beside**	**over**
against	**between**	**through**
along	**beyond**	**to the left of**
among	**by**	**to the right of**
around	**in**	**toward**
at	**inside**	**under**
before	**near**	**up**
behind	**on**	**within**

How can I make my report better?

Add a bar graph.

A **bar graph** helps the reader understand numbers you use in your writing. The bars compare two or more things. The graph below shows the number of library books read in three different classrooms during one month.

Sample Bar Graph

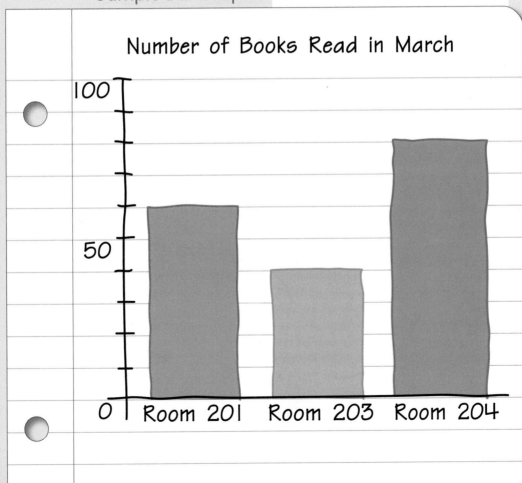

Number of Books Read in March

100

50

0   Room 201   Room 203   Room 204

Draw a diagram.

A **diagram** explains what something looks like or how it works so the reader can understand the information.

Sample Diagram

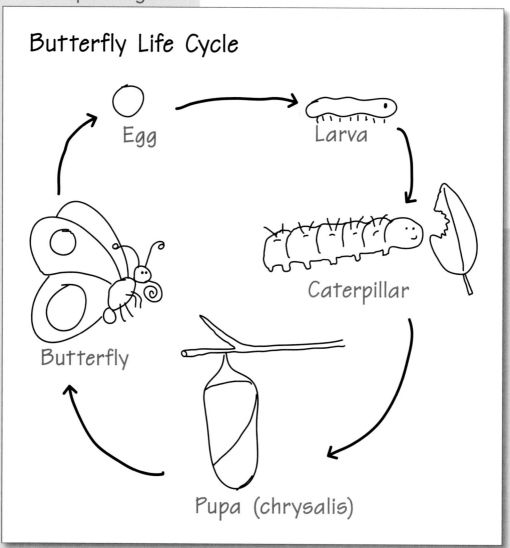

Butterfly Life Cycle

Egg

Larva

Caterpillar

Butterfly

Pupa (chrysalis)

Editing and Proofreading Marks

You can use the marks below when you revise and edit your writing. Your teacher may also use these marks to tell you how to improve your writing.

Symbol	Meaning	Example	Edited
=	Capitalize a letter.	Jean Fritz wrote *George washington's Mother.*	Jean Fritz wrote *George Washington's Mother.*
/	Make a capital letter lowercase.	George's mother was Named Mary.	George's mother was named Mary.
⊙	Add a period.	Mary baked delicious gingerbread	Mary baked delicious gingerbread.
℘	Take something out.	Her son George he joined the army.	Her son George joined the army.
∧	Add a letter, a word, or words.	Mary wished her ^son^ would stay home.	Mary wished her son would stay home.
? ! ∧ ∧ ∧	Insert punctuation.	In February of 1789∧ George was elected president.	In February of 1789, George was elected president.
sp. ⬭	Correct the spelling error.	Mary (wroot)^sp.^ letters to her son.	Mary wrote letters to her son.
#	Start a new paragraph.	Mary liked writing and reading.#One time she had . . .	Mary like writing and reading. One time she had . . .

Proofreader's Guide

Academic Vocabulary

Work with a partner. Read the meanings and share your answers.

1. **Punctuation marks** separate words and letters so that writing makes sense.
   What punctuation marks do you use?

2. An **abbreviation** is a shortened word.
   What abbreviations do you know?

3. A **series** is a number of things that come one after another.
   Name a series of things that you see.

Using
Punctuation

A **walk** signal tells you to go. A **don't walk** signal tells you to stop. These signals help you to cross the street safely.

Stopping **and** Going

Punctuation marks are signals that help you understand writing. For example, a period tells you to stop at the end of a sentence. A comma tells you to pause. This chapter will explain these and other punctuation marks.

Use a Period

At the End of a Telling Sentence

George and Martha are silly.

After an Initial

S.E. Goode

D.L. Spruce

Susan B. Anthony

After an Abbreviation

Mr. Plant

Ms. Blossom

Dr. Weed

practice
Periods

Read the sentences below. Find where a period is missing. Write the word or letters that come before the missing period and then add the period.

Example: My teacher's name is Ms Potter.

Ms.

1. Simon brings his lunch to school every day

2. His mother is Dr Brown.

3. She signs her name "Gina M Brown" on school forms.

4. Mr Brown is a carpenter.

5. Carpenters make things out of wood

6. Simon has a friend named T J Roberts.

Next Step: Write a sentence about your teacher. Include his or her name in your sentence.

Use a Question Mark

After a Question

Who sat on my lunch?

Use an Exclamation Point

After a Sentence That Shows Strong Feeling

Uh-oh, there's a skunk on the playground!

After a Word That Shows Excitement

Wow!   Help!

practice

Question Marks and Exclamation Points

Decide if each sentence below needs to end with a question mark or an exclamation point. Copy the sentences and end each with the correct punctuation mark.

Example: Hooray, the sun's coming out.

Hooray, the sun's coming out!

1. Is the storm over
2. Wow, that storm was bad
3. The wind blew so hard
4. Did the wind blow anything over
5. My bird feeder is missing
6. Was there any flooding
7. That was the scariest storm ever

Next Step: Write two sentences about a bad storm. Make one sentence a question. Make the other sentence show strong feelings.

Use a Comma

A comma looks like a period with a tail on it (,).

Between Words in a Series

I love red, purple, and silver.

In Compound Sentences

Those colors are nice, but I like the color green best of all.

(In compound sentences, the comma is put in front of the conjunctions **and, but,** and **so.**)

To Help Set Off a Speaker's Words

Russ said, "I love kickball!"

Commas 1

- **Commas in a Series**
- **Commas in Compound Sentences**

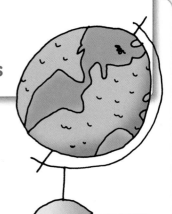

For each sentence, write the word or words that should be followed by a comma. Write the comma, too.

Example: I see Canada Mexico and the United States on this globe.

Canada, Mexico,

---

1. Juan has family in Ohio Utah and Florida.

2. Some kids in my class have been to Florida but no one has visited Utah.

3. Ashley has cousins in Ohio Texas and Maine.

4. Ashley's cousin from Maine asked her to visit so she went there last summer.

Next Step: Write a sentence about three places you'd like to visit someday.

Use a Comma

Between a City and a State
El Paso, Texas

Between the Day and the Year
May 24, 2011

After the Greeting and Closing in a Letter
Dear Grandpa,   Love,
                                Liz

After Introductory Words
When we race, J. J. likes to win.

To Name a Person Spoken to
Annie, wait for me!

Commas 2

- **Commas in Dates and Addresses**
- **Commas in Letter Writing**

Copy the friendly letter below. Add commas where they are needed.

Example: **February 2 2012**

February 2, 2012

254 Red Street
Lawton MI 49065
January 27 2012

Dear Groundhog

Please cover your eyes when you come out of your burrow this year. I am tired of winter.

Sincerely
Bruce Limm

Next Step: Write a sentence using today's date.

Use an Apostrophe

To Make a Contraction

Two Words	Contraction
do not	don't
has not	hasn't
can not	can't
she is	she's
it is	it's
I am	I'm
we will	we'll
they will	they'll
is not	isn't
will not	won't
we are	we're
they are	they're

practice

Apostrophes 1

● **Apostrophes to Make Contractions**

The two underlined words in each sentence can be made into a contraction. Write the contraction.

Example: <u>We</u> <u>will</u> go to the library.

We'll

1. We <u>do</u> <u>not</u> have to pay for books at the library.

2. <u>It</u> <u>is</u> a place where we can borrow them.

3. <u>I</u> <u>am</u> allowed to borrow books with my library card.

4. My sister Emma <u>can</u> <u>not</u> have her own library card.

5. <u>She</u> <u>is</u> just a baby!

Next Step: Use a contraction in a sentence about your school library.

Use an Apostrophe

To Show Ownership

This is Mary's book

The tree's leaves are falling.

My brother's frogs jump and croak.
(One brother owns the frogs.)

My brothers' frogs jump and croak.
(More than one brother owns the frogs.)

practice

Apostrophes 2

● **Apostrophes to Show Ownership**

For each sentence, write the possessive form of the underlined word. Then write the word that shows what the person or thing owns.

Example: The <u>bird</u> eggs are colorful.

bird's eggs

1. <u>Mom</u> ring is shiny.

2. I want to read <u>Mr. Green</u> book.

3. We found the <u>girl</u> backpack.

4. Do you know where <u>Becky</u> glasses are?

5. The <u>van</u> tire is flat.

Next Step: Write a sentence about something that belongs to your teacher. Use an apostrophe to show ownership.

Use Underlining

For Titles of Books and Magazines

I read <u>The Mouse That Snored.</u>

<u>Ranger Rick</u> comes in the mail.

Use Quotation Marks

Before and After a Speaker's Words

"I love carrots," said Sam.

practice
Underlining and Quotation Marks

Copy each sentence. Put quotation marks around a speaker's words. Underline any titles of books or magazines.

Example: Hi, Jared, said my dad.

"Hi, Jared," said my dad.

1. When are you coming home? I asked.

2. He said, I'll be home soon.

3. My dad brought me a book called Lisa's Airplane Trip.

4. Thanks, Dad, I said.

5. I read the magazine Zoobooks every month.

Next Step: Write a sentence that tells the title of a book.

Practice Test

Read each sentence. A punctuation mark is needed in each box. Write the letter that shows the correct mark.

1. Are these flowers real ☐
   Ⓐ . *(period)*   Ⓑ ❓ *(question mark)*

2. Martha said, ☐I like bananas."
   Ⓐ " *(quotation mark)*   Ⓑ ' *(apostrophe)*

3. Our Scout leader is Ms☐ Cannon.
   Ⓐ . *(period)*   Ⓑ ' *(apostrophe)*

4. I didn☐t bring my boots today.
   Ⓐ " *(quotation mark)*   Ⓑ ' *(apostrophe)*

5. We saw lions☐ monkeys, and bears at the zoo.
   Ⓐ , *(comma)*   Ⓑ ' *(apostrophe)*

6. I found Jacob☐s shoe behind the chair.
   Ⓐ , *(comma)*   Ⓑ ' *(apostrophe)*

7. Lena was born on January 14☐ 1999.
   Ⓐ , *(comma)*   Ⓑ ' *(apostrophe)*

Checking
Mechanics

Rules help you in many ways. There are rules for keeping you safe. There are rules for playing games. There are also rules for writing.

Rules for Writing

This chapter lists many rules for the **mechanics of writing**. You will learn about using capital letters, writing plurals, and much more. Following these rules helps your reader to understand what you write.

Use Capital Letters

For All Proper Nouns

Names, Titles, and Initials
➜ Jackie Wilson
Dr. Small
E. B. White

Days, Months, and Holidays
➜ Friday   January   Thanksgiving

Names of Places
➜ Canada   Rocky Mountains
Ohio   Main Street
Chicago   Sears Tower

practice

Capitalization 1

● **Proper Nouns**

Write all the words that should be capitalized in the sentences below. The number in ( ) tells how many words you should find in each sentence.

Example: We live on oak road in vicksburg. *(3)*

Oak Road, Vicksburg

---

1. Mom and I wanted to surprise Dad for father's day. *(2)*

2. We asked Dad's old friend to meet us on sunday, june 14, in austin, texas. *(4)*

3. Dad and mr. hanks grew up in austin. *(3)*

4. Now Dad lives in dallas, and mr. hanks lives in houston. *(4)*

Next Step: Write a sentence that tells the name of the place you live.

Use Capital Letters

For the First Word in a Sentence
➜ Fireflies light up the garden.

For a Speaker's First Word
Mr. Smith said, "Look at this spiderweb."

For the Word "I"
What will I say to him?

For Titles of Books, Stories, Poems, . . .
➜ Aesop's Fox (book)

"Lost in the Woods" (story)

"Elephant for Sale" (poem)

Spider (magazine)

practice

Capitalization 2

- First Words
- The Word "I"
- Titles

For each sentence, write the word or words that should be capitalized.

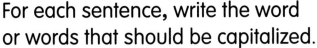

Example: my neighbor couldn't figure it out.

___My___

1. Mr. Mark said, "this shelf should fit right here!"

2. he measured the space again.

3. then he looked in a book called <u>wood works</u>.

4. Mr. Mark also looked at a magazine article called "building shelves."

5. he looked at the pictures.

6. He said, "i made a mistake!"

Next Step: What do you think Mr. Mark did wrong? Write a sentence telling about it.

Make Plurals

Add -s to make the plural of most nouns.

boy → boy**s**
shoe → shoe**s**

wing → wing**s**
book → book**s**

Add -es to make the plural of nouns ending in *s, x, sh, ch,* and *z.*

glass → glass**es**
fox → fox**es**
bush → bush**es**

inch → inch**es**
buzz → buzz**es**

Grammar practice

Plurals 1

- Most Nouns
- Nouns Ending in *ch*, *s*, *sh*, and *x*

Add **-s** or **-es** to each word to form the correct plural.

Example: pencil

pencils

1. rash

2. mess

3. flower

4. box

5. paper

6. wax

7. lunch

8. jar

Next Step: Choose one of the plurals you wrote. Write a sentence using the word.

Make Plurals

Change the word to make the plural of some nouns. These are called "irregular" plurals.

child → **children**   man → **men**

foot → **feet**   goose → **geese**

Change the _y_ to _i_ and add _-es_ to nouns that end with a consonant plus _y_.

sky → skies   story → stories

ferry → ferries   baby → babies

Grammar practice

Plurals 2

- ● **Nouns Ending in a Consonant + *y***
- ● **Irregular Plurals**

Look at the rules on page 424. Then write the correct plural form for each word below.

Example: **berry**

berries

1. woman

2. penny

3. tooth

4. bunny

5. fly

6. mouse

7. daisy

8. man

Next Step: Choose one of the plurals you wrote. Write a sentence using the word.

Use Abbreviations

For Titles of People

Mister → **Mr.**   Doctor → **Dr.**

For Days of the Week

Sunday	Sun.	Thursday	Thurs.
Monday	Mon.	Friday	Fri.
Tuesday	Tues.	Saturday	Sat.
Wednesday	Wed.		

For Months of the Year

January	Jan.	July	July
February	Feb.	August	Aug.
March	Mar.	September	Sept.
April	Apr.	October	Oct.
May	May	November	Nov.
June	June	December	Dec.

Post Office Address Abbreviations

Avenue	AVE	Road	RD
Drive	DR	South	S
East	E	Street	ST
North	N	West	W

Grammar practice

Abbreviations

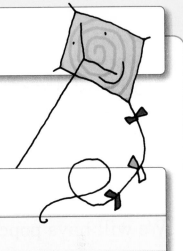

Write the abbreviation for each underlined word.

Example: <u>March</u> winds

Mar.

1. 123 OAK <u>AVENUE</u>

2. Friday, <u>August</u> 29

3. 555 STATE <u>ROAD</u>

4. <u>January</u> 3

5. 869 <u>SOUTH</u> MAIN STREET

6. Thursday, <u>September</u> 18

Next Step: Write the correct abbreviations for all the days of the week.

Grammar Practice Test

Read the paragraphs below. For each underlined part, choose the letter of the best way to write it.

      ¹
Next friday my cousin is having a party.

We will have popcorn and fruit juice. We will play
      ²
games. All my cousin will be there.

1. Ⓐ next Friday
   Ⓑ Next Friday
   Ⓒ correct as is

2. Ⓐ my cousins
   Ⓑ my Cousins
   Ⓒ correct as is

               ³
Debby's dog has six new puppys. They are
     ⁴
so cute! I wish one could be mine!

3. Ⓐ puppyes
   Ⓑ puppies
   Ⓒ correct as is

4. Ⓐ i wish
   Ⓑ I Wish
   Ⓒ correct as is

Checking
Your Spelling

The spelling list that follows on pages 430–436 is in ABC order. It includes many of the important words you will use in your writing. Check this list when you are not sure how to spell a word. (Also check a classroom dictionary for help.)

Use a Spelling Plan

1. **Look** at the word and say it.
2. **Spell** it aloud.
3. **Say** the word again, sound by sound.
4. **Notice** the spelling of each sound.
5. **Cover** the word and write it on paper.
6. **Check** the spelling.
7. If it is wrong, **repeat** the plan.

A

about
after
again
all
alone
and
animal
another
are
as
ask
aunt
away

B

back
bad
bank
be
because
been

before
bell
best
big
black
blue
boat
book
born
both
box
bright
bring
broke
brother
brown
burn
but
by

C

call
candle
card
children
clean
clock
color
come
could
cousin
crowd

D

daddy
dance
dark
dear
didn't
doesn't
dogs
doll
dollars
done
don't
door
dream
drop

practice

Spelling 1

Look at the picture in front of each phrase below. Write a word from your spelling list to fill in the blank.

Example: sails on a _____

boat

1. ● a _____ circle

2. 🔔 a ringing _____

3. 📖 an open _____

4. $ a few _____

5. ☎ make a telephone _____

6. 💧 a _____ of water

Next Step: Write a sentence using one of the phrases above.

E

each
eat
eight
end
eye

F

fall
far
fast
feather
feel
fight
fire
first
five
floor
flowers
fly
food
foot

for
forgot
found
four
Friday
friend
from
front
full
fun
funny

G

game
girl
give
going
good
grandfather
grandmother
grass
green

H

had
hair
half
hand
happen
hard
has
have
head
help
her
here
hide
high
hill
his
home
hope
horse
hot
hour
how
hurt

I

I
ice
if
I'm
is
it's
I've

J

jam
jelly
just

K

keep
kids
kind
kitten
knew

practice
Spelling 2

Write the correct word from your spelling list to fill in the blank in each sentence below.

Example: **A baby cat is called a _____.**

_kitten_____

1. The day after Thursday is _____.

2. A joke is a _____ story.

3. Frozen water is _____.

4. There are 60 minutes in an _____.

5. I raise my _____ when I want to speak in class.

Next Step: Write a sentence using another word from your spelling list.

L

lady
land
last
laugh
leave
left
letter
light
live
long
look
lot
loud
love

M

made
make
many
may
men
milk

Monday
money
monkey
month
moon
more
morning
most
mother
move
much
must
my

N

name
need
new
next
nice
night
nine
not
now

O

of
off
okay
old
once
one
open
or
orange
other
our
out

P

party
pencil
penny
play
please
poor
porch
post

pour
pretty
pull
purple

Q

quick
quiet
quit

R

rabbit
rain
read
ready
really
ride
right
road
rode
room
rope

practice
Spelling 3

Write a word from your spelling list to fill in the blanks in each sentence below. Pay attention to the hints.

Example: A r __ b __ __ __ __ has long ears.

rabbit

1. The sun does not shine at n __ __ __ h __ .

2. It rises every m __ __ n __ __ __ .

3. You may have an apple if you say
   p l __ __ __ __ .

4. Kris ate a juicy o __ __ __ __ __ __ .

5. My favorite color is p __ __ p __ __ __ .

Next Step: Write a sentence using another word from your spelling list.

S

said
Saturday
saw
say
says
school
seven
shoes
should
sister
six
sleep
soft
something
soon
sound
still
store
storm
street
summer
Sunday
sure

T

take
talk
teacher
teeth
tell
ten
thank
that
them
these
they
think
this
those
three
Thursday
told
tooth
try
Tuesday
two

U

uncle
under
until
use

V

van
very

W

walk
want
way
Wednesday
week
went
were
what
when
where

which
why
with
won
word
work
would
write

X

X-ray

Y

year
yellow
you
your
you're

Z

zipper
zoo

practice
Spelling 4

Write the correct word from your spelling list to answer each question below.

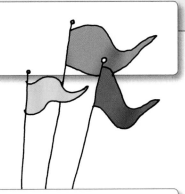

Example: How many flags are in the picture?

**three**

1. How many days are in a week?

2. Where do you go to see lions, monkeys, and bears?

3. What are the hard white things in your mouth?

4. What day comes after Tuesday?

5. What season is the hottest?

Next Step: Write a sentence using another word from your spelling list.

Practice Test

Read each sentence below. Then write the letter of the correct answer.

1. My older _____ plays games with me.
   - Ⓐ bruther
   - Ⓒ brother
   - Ⓑ bother
   - Ⓓ brothre

2. Earth's _____ comes from the sun.
   - Ⓐ lite
   - Ⓒ ligth
   - Ⓑ light
   - Ⓓ leit

3. We split the apple in _____ .
   - Ⓐ half
   - Ⓒ haf
   - Ⓑ halve
   - Ⓓ hafe

4. _____ is making a funny noise on the roof.
   - Ⓐ Sumthing
   - Ⓒ Somthing
   - Ⓑ Someting
   - Ⓓ Something

Using the
Right Word

Some words sound alike, but they have different spellings. They also have different meanings. These words are called **homophones**.

ant aunt	Mom bought me an ant farm. My aunt is my dad's sister.

ate eight	I ate a banana this morning. Shannon is eight years old.

bare bear	Look at my bare feet! The grizzly bear growled.

blew
blue

Dakota blew the biggest bubble.

A robin's egg is blue.

by
buy

Place the spoon by the knife.

We must buy some milk today.

dear
deer

My grandma is a dear woman.

The deer ran into the woods.

for
four

Miss Nelson made lunch for us.

Nick ate four tacos.

practice

Using the Right Word

- blew, blue
- buy, by
- dear, deer
- for, four

For each sentence, write the correct
word from the choice given.

Example: Jimmy *(blew, blue)* into the whistle toy.

> blew

1. It was his *(dear, deer)* grandma's birthday!

2. She told Jimmy not to *(buy, by)* a gift.

3. He made a painting *(for, four)* her.

4. He used a lot of *(blew, blue)* paint.

5. He painted a *(dear, deer)* with antlers.

6. He painted *(for, four)* kinds of flowers, too.

Next Step: Write a sentence telling about a picture
you would like to paint. Use the word *by*
in your sentence.

hear
here

I like to hear birds sing.

Who sits here?

its
it's

The dog ate its food.

I think it's about 8:00.

(it's = it is)

knew
new

I knew my ABC's last year.

We have a new girl in our class.

know
no

Do you know her name?

Robert said, "No, I don't."

practice
Using the Right Word 2
- ● **hear, here**
- ● **knew, new**
- ● **its, it's**
- ● **know, no**

Write the correct word for each sentence.

> Example: I have a *(knew, new)* joke to tell you.
>
> ___new___

1. Maxine, are you ready to *(hear, here)* it?

2. *(Its, It's)* about bees going to school.

3. Do you *(know, no)* how they get there?

4. Maxine said, "*(Know, No)*, tell me."

5. A bee gets to school on *(its, it's)* buzz.

6. She laughed and said, "I *(knew, new)* it would be a funny one!"

Next Step: Write a sentence telling how you get to school. Use one of the blue words at the top of the page in your sentence.

one
won

My baby brother is one year old.

Liz won a prize at the fair.

their
there
they're

We used their bikes.
(Their shows ownership.)

There are four of them.

They're mountain bikes.
(they're = they are)

to
two
too

I like to read funny books.

I read two joke books today.

Joe likes joke books, too.

practice

Using the Right Word 3

- one, won
- their, there, they're
- to, two, too

Write the correct word for
each sentence.

Example: Mom *(one, won)* a fruit basket as a
prize at the school carnival.

_**won**_____

1. The basket had *(one, won)* apple in it.

2. It had bananas, *(to, too, two)*.

3. *(Their, There, They're)* were some cherries, too.

4. Mom is going *(to, too, two)* make a fruit salad.

5. Dad will eat *(to, too, two)* bowls of fruit.

Next Step: Write a sentence about winning a prize.
Use the word *their* in your sentence.

Antonyms

Antonyms are two words with opposite meanings. Here are some common antonyms you should know.

above	—	below
clean	—	dirty
day	—	night
fast	—	slow
first	—	last
happy	—	sad
hard	—	soft
high	—	low
hot	—	cold
laugh	—	cry
left	—	right
loud	—	quiet
on	—	off
push	—	pull
short	—	tall
up	—	down
win	—	lose

practice

Antonyms

Finish each sentence below with the opposite (antonym) of the word under the line.

Example: Matthew's house is on the _____ side of the street.
(left)

_____right_____

1. Yesterday it was _____ outside.
   (cold)

2. The teacher asked the children to be _____.
   (loud)

3. It's too bad we did not _____ this game.
   (lose)

4. Someone left the light _____.
   (off)

5. I like my pillow. It is not too _____.
   (hard)

Next Step: Write a sentence like those above. Use any pair of antonyms that was not used here.

Practice Test

Choose the right word to complete each sentence. Write the letter **A** or **B** on your paper.

1. The bear took our food in _____ mouth.
   Ⓐ its   Ⓑ it's

2. The antonym for *on* is _____ .
   Ⓐ of   Ⓑ off

3. The Bitville Tigers _____ the game.
   Ⓐ won   Ⓑ one

4. We'll have our picnic _____ at the park.
   Ⓐ hear   Ⓑ here

5. It is too wet on the ground over _____ .
   Ⓐ their   Ⓑ there

6. The antonym for *down* is _____ .
   Ⓐ up   Ⓑ below

7. Leon will watch the movie, _____ .
   Ⓐ to   Ⓑ too

Understanding
Sentences

A **sentence** tells a complete idea and has two parts.

    1. The **subject** is the naming part.
    2. The **predicate** (verb) is the telling part.

The verb tells what the subject is doing.

    My <u>mom</u> <u>rides</u> a motorcycle.
       subject verb

A **sentence** begins with a capital letter. It ends with a period, a question mark, or an exclamation point.

    Grandpa climbs trees.
    Can he reach the top?
    Wow, he is way up there!

The Subject

The **subject** is the naming part of a sentence. It tells who or what the sentence is about. A subject is usually a noun that names a person, place, or thing.

My new baby **sister** sleeps a lot.
(*Sister* is the main word in the subject.)

My new baby sister sleeps a lot.
(*My new baby sister* are all the words in the subject.)

The subject can also be a pronoun.
She went to the mall.
It is a new car.
We will listen to music.

Subject of a Sentence

For each sentence, write the complete subject.

> Example: **An explorer waved his map around.**
>
> _An explorer_

1. The explorer's shirt was striped.
2. He wore a patch on one eye.
3. His old, torn map led to a chest.
4. A dotted line showed the way.
5. The chest could hold gold.
6. It could hold a very old book or a vase.

Next Step: Write a sentence about what kind of buried treasure the explorer found. Underline the complete subject.

The Predicate

The **predicate** is the telling part of a sentence. It contains the **verb**. The predicate either tells what the subject is doing, or it tells something about the subject.

My uncle Benny **builds** doghouses.
(*Builds* is the verb in the predicate.)

My uncle Benny **builds doghouses.**
(*Builds doghouses* is the complete predicate.)

That flower **is beautiful.**
(The verb *is* and the word *beautiful* form the complete predicate. This predicate tells something about the subject.)

Grammar practice
Predicate of a Sentence

For each sentence, write the complete predicate.

> Example: The stoplight turned red.
>
> _turned red_

1. Mom stopped the car.

2. Two kids pressed the *walk* button.

3. They crossed the street.

4. They were very careful.

5. The light changed to green.

6. They went on their way.

Next Step: Write a sentence about a car trip. Underline the complete predicate.

Kinds of Sentences

A **telling sentence** makes a statement.

Soccer is my favorite game.

An **asking sentence** asks a question.

Will you play with me?

A **command sentence** makes a request or gives directions.

Kick with the side of your foot.

An **exclamatory sentence** shows surprise or strong feelings.

Watch out for the ball!

Grammar practice
Kinds of Sentences

Write a letter for each sentence.
Write **T** for telling, **A** for asking,
E for exclamatory, and **C** for command.

Example: How do birds stay dry when it rains?

A

1. Feathers protect a bird from getting too wet.

2. Wow, some birds cannot fly!

3. Do you have a pet bird at home?

4. Clean its cage often.

5. My aunt has a myna bird.

6. Can a myna "talk" better than a parrot?

Next Step: Write a sentence about a bird. Ask a
classmate to tell what kind of sentence
you have written.

Grammar Practice Test

Read the sentences below. Look at the part of the sentence that is underlined. Write the letter that names the underlined part.

1. John <u>plays the piano</u>.
   Ⓐ subject   Ⓑ predicate

2. <u>Our music teacher</u> is the best!
   Ⓐ subject   Ⓑ predicate

Read each sentence. Write the letter that tells what kind of sentence it is.

1. Watch out for the bees!
   Ⓐ telling sentence   Ⓑ exclamatory sentence

2. Kerry plays soccer on Saturdays.
   Ⓐ telling sentence   Ⓑ command sentence

3. Do you like swimming lessons?
   Ⓐ exclamatory sentence   Ⓑ asking sentence

4. Tara, close the door.
   Ⓐ asking sentence   Ⓑ command sentence

Using the
Parts of Speech

All of the words you use fit into eight groups. These groups are called the **parts of speech**.

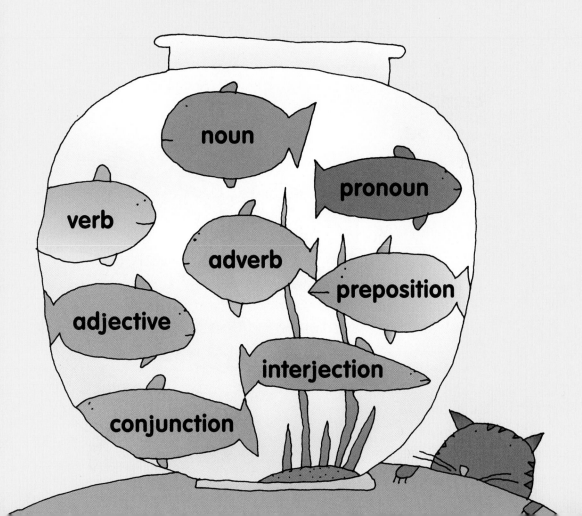

Nouns

A **noun** is a word that names a person, place, or thing.

person:	girl	firefighter
place:	house	school
thing:	bike	flower

Nouns can be **common** or **proper**.

common:	boy	street
proper:	Gus	Oak Street

Nouns 1

● **Common and Proper Nouns**

Write the nouns you find in each sentence. (The number of nouns in each sentence is given at the end of the sentence.) Underline the proper nouns.

> Example: Tito and his family are planning a trip. *(3)*
>
> _Tito, family, trip_

1. Tito wants to swim in the Pacific Ocean. *(2)*

2. Val would like to see the Rocky Mountains. *(2)*

3. Ricky likes beaches. *(2)*

4. Their dad likes campgrounds in Vermont. *(3)*

5. Mrs. Rodriguez wants to rest at the beach. *(2)*

Next Step: Write a sentence about a trip you would like to take. Ask a classmate to underline each noun in your sentence.

Nouns

Nouns can be **singular** or **plural**.
   singular: neighbor   house
   plural: neighbors   houses

A **possessive noun** shows ownership.
Add **'s** after a singular noun.

   Julie's flute

   the **bird's** wings

Add only an apostrophe (') after most plural nouns.

   The **boys'** camp is near the lake.

   There were eggs in both **birds'** nests.

Nouns 2

- **Singular and Plural Nouns**
- **Possessive Nouns**

Make two columns. Write the singular nouns from the paragraph below in one column. Write the plural nouns in the other column.

Example: **Pamela watered the plants.**

Singular	Plural
Pamela	plants

Hank likes Mr. Green's garden. Mr. Green asked Hank and Pamela to help him. They dug a little hole for each seed. They planted tomatoes and potatoes. They also planted beans, peas, carrots, and onions. When they harvest their crops, they will have a big meal at Hasheem's house.

Next Step: Read the paragraph again. Write down two possessive nouns that you find.

Pronouns

A **pronoun** is a word that takes the place of a noun. Here are some pronouns.

singular:

I	my	your	her	him	it
me	you	she	he	his	its

plural:

we	you	our	them
us	your	they	their

Pronouns stand for nouns in sentences.

(*She* stands for *Holly.*)

Holly played a game.
She hid the penny.

(*He* stands for *Erik. It* stands for *kite.*)

Erik made a kite.
Then he flew it.

Grammar practice

Pronouns

For each sentence below, write the pronoun. Then write the noun it stands for.

Example: The bird broke its wing.

its — bird

1. Rena braids her long hair.

2. Davon, you may have a snack.

3. Mom made dinner, and the family enjoyed it.

4. Ted said, "My backpack is heavy."

5. Luke and Kenny raised their hands at the same time.

6. The teacher saw Luke first and picked him.

Next Step: Write one or two sentences about a friend. Use a pronoun to take the place of a noun.

Verbs

A **verb** is a word that shows action or helps complete a thought (linking verb).

Spot **barks** at my neighbor. (action verb)

Mr. Wilson **is** so mad! (linking verb)

Common Linking Verbs:

is	are	was	been
were	am	be	

Some Action Verbs:

ask	fix	jump	play
cook	help	listen	ride
dance	hug	move	stop

Grammar practice

Verbs 1

● **Action and Linking Verbs**

Write the verb in each sentence below. Then write **A** for action or **L** for linking.

Example: Katy listens to her CD.

listens, A

1. She owns a CD player.

2. Katy likes country music.

3. Her favorite song is "Country Mile."

4. Sometimes she dances to the music.

5. She is a good dancer.

6. Katy also sings well.

Next Step: Write one or two sentences about the kind of music you like. Underline the verb or verbs.

Verb Tenses

Some verbs tell what is happening now, or in the **present**.

Sarah **walks** her dog every morning.

Some verbs tell what happened in the **past**.

Sarah **walked** her dog last night.

(Many verbs in our language are **regular**. This means you add -*ed* to form the past tense.)

Some verbs tell what will happen in the **future**.

Sarah **will walk** her dog tomorrow.

Verbs 2

- ● Verb Tenses

Write the action verb in each sentence below. Then write **present, past,** or **future.**

Example: I save money in my piggy bank.

_____save, present_____

1. Tina saved more than six dollars last month.

2. She puts all her change in a pretty box.

3. Jane will buy a new baseball glove.

4. Her brother tossed the ball to Jane.

5. She wants a catcher's mitt.

6. The baseball season will start in a few weeks.

Next Step: Write a sentence about saving money. What verb tense did you use?

Irregular Verbs

Some verbs are **irregular**. You usually can't add -ed to them. They change in different ways.

Present Tense	Past Tense	With Helping Verb
am, is, are	was, were	been
begin	began	begun
break	broke	broken
catch	caught	caught
come	came	come
draw	drew	drawn
eat	ate	eaten
fall	fell	fallen
give	gave	given
go	went	gone
hide	hid	hidden, hid
know	knew	known
ride	rode	ridden
run	ran	run
see	saw	seen
sing	sang, sung	sung
take	took	taken
throw	threw	thrown
write	wrote	written

Grammar practice

Verbs 3

● **Irregular Verbs**

Read each sentence below. Complete each with the past tense of the verb in parentheses. (Look on page 468 for help.)

Example: A friendly cat _____ to our door. *(come)*

came

1. We _____ her some milk and food. *(give)*

2. The cat _____ it all up. *(eat)*

3. Then she _____ our dog. *(see)*

4. The cat quickly _____ into the bushes. *(run)*

5. She _____ there for a long time. *(hide)*

Next Step: Write a sentence about an animal. Use the past tense form of an irregular verb.

Adjectives

An **adjective** is a word that describes a noun or pronoun.

Large snakes live in the jungle.

An anaconda is a giant one!

The words *a, an,* and *the* are **articles**.
Use *a* before a consonant sound:

a parrot

Use *an* before a vowel sound:

an otter

Grammar practice

Adjectives 1

● Adjectives and Articles

Write the adjectives and articles from each sentence below. The number in ( ) tells you how many you will find.

Example: The old airplane flew in circles. *(2)*

The, old

1. The plane made loud noises. *(2)*

2. It left long trails of white smoke. *(2)*

3. The smoke looked like huge letters. *(2)*

4. The little plane was writing! *(2)*

5. The blue sky had a funny message. *(4)*

Next Step: Write a sentence that tells what the plane wrote. Use adjectives and articles.

Adjectives That Compare

An **adjective** sometimes compares two nouns
(or pronouns).

An ant is **smaller** than an anaconda.

A lion's roar is **louder** than a cat's meow.

An **adjective** can also compare more than
two nouns.

The anteater is the **oddest** animal in our zoo.

The **biggest** mammal in the world is the whale.

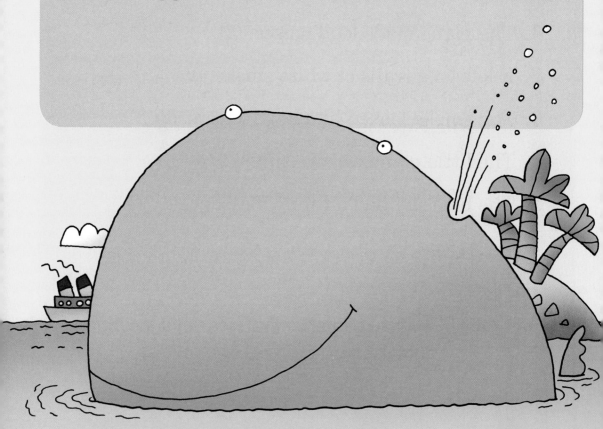

Adjectives 2

● **Adjectives That Compare**

For each sentence, write the correct adjective.

> Example: An elephant is *(bigger, biggest)* than a hippo.
>
> **bigger**

1. The *(hotter, hottest)* place in the United States is Death Valley.

2. A cheetah is the *(faster, fastest)* animal on land.

3. The Nile River is *(longer, longest)* than the Ohio River.

4. Jill has the *(darker, darkest)* hair of anyone in our class.

5. My dog is *(smaller, smallest)* than Ken's dog.

Next Step: Write a sentence that includes an adjective that compares.

Adverbs

An **adverb** is a word that describes a verb.
It can tell *how, where,* or *when.*

How:	Erin ran quickly.
Where:	She fell down.
When:	She has fallen before.

Here are some other adverbs.

How:	brightly	carefully	easily
	fast	loudly	quietly
Where:	away	forward	nearby
	outside	there	upstairs
When:	always	first	often
	weekly	yearly	yesterday

Grammar practice

Adverbs

Write the adverb you find in each sentence below. Hint: Look for the action verb first.

> Example: The fish swam away.
>
> _____away_____

1. Teddy quietly read his book.

2. We went swimming yesterday.

3. Mom slowly added milk to the gravy.

4. Sunflowers grow fast.

5. Donna walks there.

6. The airplane glided smoothly to a stop.

Next Step: Write a sentence that uses an adverb.

Prepositions, Conjunctions, and Interjections

A **preposition** is used to help make a statement.

Maya laughed **at** the joke.

A **prepositional phrase** begins with a preposition.

Maya laughed **at the joke**.

A **conjunction** connects words or ideas.

I will dance **or** sing.

First I cried, **and** then I laughed.

An **interjection** shows excitement.

Wow! Did you see that bug?

Yuck! I hate creepy crawlers!

Grammar
practice
Prepositions, Conjunctions, and Interjections

Write the correct word to complete
each sentence.

Example: *(Wow, Oh no)*, Isabel is a good
cheerleader!

Wow

Prepositions

1. Jake ran *(up, in)* the stairs.

2. We can walk *(on, to)* the store.

Conjunctions

3. I can choose a pear *(or, but)* an apple.

4. Ned's family has a cat *(so, and)* a dog.

Interjections

5. Marvin scared me when he said, "*(Boo, Gosh)*!"

Next Step: Write a sentence that shows excitement.
Use an interjection.

Grammar Practice Test

For each underlined word in the following sentences, write the letter that shows what part of speech it is.

1. Kate wrote a <u>poem</u>.
   Ⓐ noun   Ⓑ pronoun   Ⓒ adverb

2. Are <u>you</u> a student at this school?
   Ⓐ noun   Ⓑ pronoun   Ⓒ verb

3. The flower <u>bends</u> in the wind.
   Ⓐ noun   Ⓑ verb   Ⓒ adverb

4. A <u>huge</u> cloud hid the sun.
   Ⓐ adjective   adverb   Ⓒ noun

5. Robbie stood <u>outside</u>.
   Ⓐ adverb   Ⓑ interjection   Ⓒ verb

6. It started to rain <u>in</u> the morning.
   Ⓐ preposition   Ⓑ conjunction   Ⓒ adjective

7. I like to read <u>and</u> draw.
   Ⓐ adjective   Ⓑ preposition   Ⓒ conjunction

Credits

Text:
P. 269, Copyright © 2003 by Houghton Mifflin Harcourt Publishing Company. Adapted and reproduced by permission from *The American Heritage First Dictionary*.

Photos:
270 ©Comstock/Getty Images; 271 bottom ©Corbis; 271 center ©Hemera Technologies/JupiterImages; 271 top ©Photodisc/Getty Images

Index

The index will help you find specific information in this book. Words that are in italics are from the "Using the Right Word" section. The colored boxes contain information you will use often.

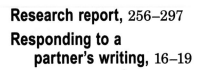